WHEN THE COMFORTER CAME

When the Comforter Came

A 31-Day Devotional
on the Holy Spirit

A.B. SIMPSON

CHRISTIAN PUBLICATIONS
CAMP HILL, PENNSYLVANIA

Christian Publications
3825 Hartzdale Drive, Camp Hill, PA 17011

The mark of ⊹ vibrant faith

ISBN: 0-87509-469-4
LOC Catalog Card Number: 91-73585
© 1991 by Christian Publications
All rights reserved
Printed in the United States of America

91 92 93 94 95   5 4 3 2 1

Cover Photo: Comstock

CONTENTS

ORPHANED LIVES

I will not leave you as orphans;
I will come to you. (John 14:18)

A few years ago a striking Christmas card was published, with the title "If He had not come." It was founded upon our Savior's own words "If I had not come" (John 15:22). The card represented a clergyman falling into a short sleep in his study on Christmas morning and dreaming of a world into which Jesus had never come. In his dream he found himself looking through his home but there were no little stockings in the chimney corner, no Christmas bells or wreaths of holly, and no Christ to comfort, gladden and save. He walked out on the public street but there was no church with its spire pointing to heaven. He came back and sat down in his library but every book about the Savior and the gospel had disappeared. A ring came to the door bell and a messenger asked him to visit a poor dying mother. He hastened with her weeping child and as he reached the home he sat down and said, "I have something here that I am sure will comfort you." He opened his Bible to look for a familiar promise but it ended at Malachi and there was no gospel and no promise of hope and salvation, and he could only bow his head and weep with her in bitter despair. Two days afterwards he stood beside her coffin and conducted the funeral service, but there was no message of consolation, no word of a glorious resurrection, no open heaven, but only "dust to dust, ashes to ashes," and one long eternal farewell. He realized at length that "He had not come" and burst into tears and bitter weeping in his sorrowful dream. Suddenly he awoke with a start and a great shout of joy and praise burst from his lips as he heard his choir singing in the church close by:

> Oh! come all ye faithful, joyful and
>   triumphant,
> In Bethlehem's manger lies the King of
>   Angels.
> Oh! come let us adore Him Christ
>   the Lord.

This striking illustration suggests to us something of what we would have missed if the Holy Spirit had not come. There could have been no

Comforter and no comfort. The work which our Lord accomplished at so much cost could never have been completed. There could have been no conviction of sin, no repentance, no faith in the Lord Jesus Christ, no sense of forgiven sin, no balm of peace for the troubled conscience, no "Spirit of sonship . . . crying 'Abba Father'" (Romans 8:15b), no revelation of Jesus Christ to the heart, no sanctification from the power of sin, no Spirit of intercession to help us and teach us to pray, no power to anoint us for our Christian work, no supernatural presence in our Christian life and in the life and work of the Church of God. All this would have been lacking if the Spirit had not come and our hearts would be orphaned indeed.

An orphan is one who has had a parent, a mother, a home and all the sweetness and help of fostering love and care, and lost it. The disciples of Christ were in this very condition. The Lord had been a Teacher, a Guide, a Friend and a spiritual mother. And now He was to leave them, and to leave them utterly unfitted for their lonely and orphaned condition. Their knowledge as yet was dim, their faith was feeble, they were little children who had scarcely learned to walk alone, and it was with utter consternation that they heard Him say He was going away. How could they ever face the world alone, lambs in the midst of wolves, orphans in a hostile homeless wilderness?

He has not failed to mark their anxious faces

and their falling tears and He hastens to reassure them, "I will not leave you as orphans" (John 14:18a). And then He adds something that it must have been hard for them at first to understand after what He had already told them about His going away. "I will come to you" (18b), He says. But how could He come to them if He was going to leave them? And then He proceeds to explain to them that the One who is to succeed Him, the Presence that is to take His place and abide with them forever is just His own very Self in another form, the Spiritual Christ, the Heart of Jesus returning to abide with us forever, just as really as when He walked in Galilee and yet in a manner wholly different and infinitely better.

"On that day," He says, "You will realize that I am in the Father and you are in me and I am in you" (John 14:20). The coming of the Comforter is to make Jesus intensely real, more real indeed than the Comforter Himself. "He will testify about me" (John 15:26b). "The Spirit will take from what is mine and make it known to you" (John 16:15b). Still further He assures them that through the coming of the Comforter He will manifest Himself to the heart of each disciple and He and the Father together "will come to him and make our home with him" (John 14:23b).

There is a subtle danger that in our theological conception of the glorious Trinity we sometimes make three Gods instead of one. While there are three Persons in the Godhead, yet there is one divine Presence which the Holy Spirit brings to the heart and that is the Presence of the Lord Jesus who is to us the Living Word and the one eternal Revelation of the Father. Let us not fail to grasp this precious truth that as Jesus Christ while on earth never did anything without the Holy Spirit, so now the Holy Spirit never does anything apart from Jesus. The coming of the Comforter, therefore, to the heart means the indwelling and abiding of the Lord Jesus Himself as our ever present all-sufficient and everlasting Friend.

Alas! how many of the Father's children are as yet strangers to His manifested presence, and orphans indeed! Poor orphaned hearts, the heart of Jesus is calling you to His love and fellowship and the fullness of the blessed Holy Ghost. All that your heart has ever known of fatherhood, motherhood or home, God is waiting to give to you through the indwelling of the blessed Comforter. Will you answer to His call even as you read these lines?

> Jesus, without Thee we're orphaned and
>   lonely,
> Come as our Teacher and Guide;
> Leave us not comfortless, send us the
>   Comforter,
> Come to our hearts to abide.

SOMETHING BETTER THAN HIS PRESENCE

*But I tell you the truth: It is for your good
that I am going away.* (John 16:7a)

How could anything be better for them than
the continued presence of the Master? And
yet He tells them that He is going to send them
something better than if He Himself should still
remain with them. Surely such an announcement
must have staggered them, as much as if a mother
were to tell her babes that her death would be a
positive benefit to her orphaned children.

Have we not sometimes thought and wished
that Jesus Christ were here on earth again and felt
if only we could go to His blessed feet and pour

into His living ears the story of our sorrow, it would bring us a realization of His help and presence that now we cannot know. And yet if our text be true Jesus has given us something better in the Holy Spirit than even His own visible and bodily presence among us could ever be. Oh! how this should enhance our realization of the preciousness of the Holy Spirit, that the Lord Himself says He is of more value to us than the presence of Jesus in visible and bodily form.

A little reflection will show us that the Master was right and was not exaggerating when He said, "It is for your good that I am going away. Unless I go away, the Counselor will not come to you" (John 16:7a). Let us bear in mind as we follow this train of thought that the Holy Spirit identifies Himself with the Lord Jesus and that the coming of the Comforter is just the coming of Jesus Himself to the heart.

In the first place if Jesus had continued with them in visible form He could only have been in one place at one time and His presence would have been local and individual. He could not have spoken to one here and another on the other side of the world. But now in His spiritual Presence He is omnipresent and able to give His whole attention to you, and at the same moment be in conscious fellowship with innumerable other hearts in all the world. There is nothing more wonderful than this universal Christ and His strange and unlimited power to give to us the sense of His undivided interest in us and His whole thought, attention and care for us and all we have to tell Him, while at the same moment innumerable other souls are claiming His interest and pouring their needs and sorrows into His ear. Yes, we do thank Him that He has come back to us in this larger sense and this more universal and worldwide presence.

In the second place if Jesus had still remained with them He could only have communicated with them through His outward touch. His messages would still have been addressed through imperfect human language to their ears and understanding and it would have been an external presence and communion. But now He meets us in our deeper and higher nature by the communion of His Spirit without mind and spirit, not only in actual words and thoughts but in those inarticulate and inexpressible influences and impulses which no words could ever fully convey. The presence of Christ and the fellowship of His life and love are "immeasurably more than all" that words could speak or heart could think. He imparts to us His very life and feeds us with the living Bread. He breathes into us the sweetness of His peace that passes all understanding. He sheds abroad in our hearts the love of God. He rolls upon us the burden of His prayer and the fellowship of His sufferings. He even pours into our mortal frame the fullness of His resurrection life, healing our sick and suffering bodies and vitalizing all our being with His life and strength. All this and infinitely more could never have been if

Jesus had not gone away and then come back to us through the presence of the Comforter.

Dear friend, have you come to know in this deep spiritual way the spiritual and everpresent Christ? And do you recognize the Holy Spirit as the Spirit of Jesus and in His blessed presence in your heart do you meet your beloved Lord? It was for this reason that the Holy Spirit came upon Jesus and resided in Him during His earthly ministry. All the works that Jesus did were done through the energy of the Holy Spirit. His preaching and teaching were through the anointing of the Holy Ghost. His miracles were wrought through the power of the Spirit's words. His acts of tenderness and love were the manifestations of the gentle heart of the Holy Ghost. And now that Spirit that dwelt in Him has come forth from Him to dwell in us and be to us the very heart of Christ Himself.

A thoughtful writer has reminded us that the Holy Ghost does not now come to us only as the Spirit of the Father and with that majesty and glory which the Old Testament representations of God inspire, but rather as the Spirit of Jesus and clothed with all the tenderness of His humanity. The Spirit has no material body like Jesus, the Son of God, who became incarnate in mortal flesh, but yet, in another sense, the Spirit did become incarnate in Jesus, and now comes to us softened and humanized by His union with the Lord Jesus Christ. Blessed Spirit of Christ! Let us receive Him. Let us love Him. Let us trust Him.

And let us recognize in Him that other divine Personality who must ever be to the believer's heart the sweetest of all names and the dearest of all friends, Jesus our Beloved Lord.

Yes, He is with us still, "all the days even unto the end of the age."

> What though His holy footsteps
> Linger no longer here?
> Still through His Spirit's presence
> Jesus is ever near.
> What though your heart be lonely,
> What though your friends be few,
> He will not leave you orphans,
> Jesus will come to you.

Third Day

THE MOTHER-
HOOD OF GOD

*As a mother comforts a child so I will com-
fort you; and you will be comforted over
Jerusalem.* (Isaiah 66:13)

T he tendency of the human heart to look for
something in God answering to womanly
tenderness and maternal love is illustrated by the
strong hold which Mariolatry or the worship of
the Virgin has always had upon the Roman
Catholic mind. The ignorant and superstitious
feel that in a woman's sympathy they can look for
something which not even the love of Jesus Himself fully satisfies. They do not understand that
the heart of Christ is not only the heart of a man
but has in it also all the tenderness and gentleness
of woman. Jesus was not a man in the rigid sense

11

of manhood as distinct from womanhood, but, as the Son of Man, the complete Head of humanity, He combined in Himself the nature both of man and women even as the first man Adam had the women within his own being before she was separately formed from his very body.

Back even in the Old Testament we find God revealing Himself under the sweet figure of motherhood. "As a mother comforts a child so I will comfort you." And this aspect of His blessed character finds its perfect manifestation in the Holy Ghost, our Mother God. So that we have in the divine Trinity not only a Father, and a Brother and a Husband but also One who meets all the heart's longing for motherhood.

The beautiful figure which the Lord Jesus used in John 14:18, "I will not leave you as orphans," covers this suggestion of motherhood. The Comforter as our spiritual Mother is the author of our being and gives us our new and heavenly birth. We are born of the Holy Spirit, our very life comes to us through the quickening life of the Holy Ghost.

As our heavenly Mother, the Comforter assumes our nature, training, teaching, and the whole direction of our life. All this is in accordance with the Master's words explaining the mission of the Spirit. "He will guide you into all truth" (John 16:13b), "He will teach you all things and will remind you of everything I have said to you" (John 14:26b), "I have much more to say to you, more than you can now bear. But when he, the Spirit of truth, comes, He will guide you into all truth" (John 15:12–13b). The special feature of the Spirit's teaching and guiding is its considerate gentleness and patience. He does not force upon us truth for which we are not yet prepared but leads us tenderly and teaches us, as He Himself has expressed it in the Old Testament, "line upon line, precept upon precept, here a little and there a little" (Isaiah 28:10, KJV).

The ancient teacher in classic times was quite different from our modern schoolmaster. He was the companion and friend of his disciples. They walked with him here and there all the day long on the street, in the marketplace, in the fields and on the highway and everything they saw and heard was turned to account and became the subject of conversation and illustration. So He teaches, using everything that comes in our experience as an object lesson and occasion for some new truth in Christian living. So the Comforter waits until we have learned one lesson well and are able to pass on to a higher class and a profounder truth. So He brings to our remembrance forgotten messages, and goes over again with us the lessons we have not yet fully learned, with infinite patience and unwearied pains.

But it is when the hour of trouble comes that we most need the touch of a mother's hand and the solace of a mother's love. We go to other friends when everything is bright and comfortable, but to our mother of whom we say,

Who ran to help when I fell,
And would some pretty story tell,
Or kiss the place to make it well?
My mother!

The Bible has much to say about comfort. God is "the God of all comfort" and it is the Holy Spirit that administers His loving kindness and divine consolation. The Christian life is an experience of trial and sorrow and we are always needing sympathy and consolation. How sweetly the Spirit comforts!

And true motherhood does not leave out the discipline and faithful reproof which erring childhood so often needs. Well may we ask,

Do you think He ne'er reproves me?
What a false Friend He would be.

And so the Holy Spirit loves us with such inexorable love that He would rather cause us pain than let us miss our way. Sometimes He hides His face and withdraws His conscious presence until we learn our lesson and seek His forgiveness with penitence, surrender and obedience and sweetly learn the truth that "No discipline seems pleasant at the time, but painful. Later on, however, it produces a harvest of righteousness and peace for those who have been trained by it" (Hebrews 12:11).

Fourth Day

THE HEAVENLY DOVE

*I saw the Spirit come down from heaven as
a dove and remain on Him.* (John 1:32)

The figure of motherhood referred to in the last chapter suggests the oldest emblem of the Comforter in the Bible, the figure of the dove. We find it in the second verse of the first chapter of Genesis, "The Spirit of God was . . . brooding . . . over the waters" (Amplified). The metaphor here is obviously that of the mother bird, slowly and patiently incubating her brood. The Holy Spirit is the great Mother heart and Source of life both in the physical, intellectual and spiritual world and is here bringing into being the vital forces and the living organisms of the new earth. The figure finely represents the

15

patient love of the Holy Ghost in brooding over the darkness of the human soul and bringing to birth the first throbs of spiritual life.

Perhaps there is no figure in the natural world more touching than that of the mother bird, patiently brooding through the long days and the lonely nights with no sign of responsive life over the cold and silent germs beneath her wings, and then rejoicing over the little fledglings and nurturing them with infinite tenderness until they are strong enough to be independent of her care. Surely this is a divine type of that infinite love that seeks the lost soul, that waits through long rejection and cold insensibility, until at last the first spark of heavenly life appears and the spirit is born from above in conviction, conversion and trust.

The same ancient figure also sets forth the processes and the operations of the Spirit in every new experience of our Christian life in leading us into the revelation of our sinfulness and the experience of His sanctifying grace. The Spirit has often to brood long over the dark waters of our sinful hearts. And in the equally distinct and divine process of quickening our mortal bodies and revealing in us the healing power of Christ we must learn to expect the same gradual processes and the same patient and untiring love.

The most pronounced suggestion of this beautiful figure of the Spirit is peace. The Holy Spirit comes to us as the pledge of peace with God through the finished work of the Lord Jesus

Christ. This was beautifully set forth in the ancient story of the return of Noah's dove to the ark with an olive branch in its mouth as proof that the judgment was past and that God was again ready to give to men reconciliation and grace. The Holy Spirit brings that deeper peace which comes from heart union with God Himself and the indwelling of the Comforter in the sanctuary of the soul.

The charm of His heavenly peace is that it is not dependent upon outward conditions, but is often most manifest when every circumstance is disturbing and distracting. A competition was once held for a prize to be given to the most original allegorical painting of peace. One artist brought a landscape of exquisite beauty and tranquility, the limpid lake, the softly flowing brook, the green fields with cattle and sheep feeding on the rich pasture, luxuriant trees with birds singing in the branches and children playing under their shadow, while soft fleecy clouds sailed across the blue expanse and flung their changing shadows on the mountain sides. It was indeed a perfect picture of peace under normal conditions. But the painting that won the prize was very different. It represented a naked rock in midocean with wild tempests beating around it and the surf tossing high about its base while a ship in distress was seen driving before the fierce hurricane, and the clouds were black and angry with the fury of the storm. But in the center of the picture that naked rock was seen to divide near the summit, and, in its cleft, a dove was calmly dropping into her nest and spreading her soft wings above her little brood, safe and quiet amid all the fury of the elements. That is "the peace which transcends all understanding," and is above all reasoning or understanding.

> There is a peace that cometh after sorrow,
> Of hope abandoned, not of hope fulfilled;
> That looks not out upon a glad tomorrow
> But on a tempest which His hand has stilled.
>
> A peace that dwells in solitude secluded,
> From every storm and strife of passion free;
> Tis not the peace that over Eden brooded
> But that which triumphed in Gethsemane.

It was as a dove that the Holy Spirit descended upon Jesus. This must ever make the emblem of the dove peculiarly dear to every Christian heart. The same baptism that fell upon the Master awaits all His followers who yield themselves, like Him, in full consecration to the will of God. How gently that baptism fell! As truly and fully we also may receive the descending Dove who is more willing to become our Guest that we can be to receive Him.

> Holy Ghost, I bid Thee welcome,
> Come and be my holy Guest,
> Heavenly Dove, within my bosom
> Make Thy home and build Thy nest.

Fifth Day

THE LOVE OF THE SPIRIT

I urge you . . . by the love of the Spirit.
(Romans 15:30)

We say much of the Father's love and the wonderful love of Jesus, but do we fully realize and appreciate the love of the Spirit?

1. The very fact that the Holy Spirit has left the love and joy of heaven and made His residence for nearly 2000 years in this uncongenial world, places His sacrifice alongside that of Jesus Christ in His incarnation and redemption. Indeed that sacrifice of the third Person of the Trinity has been a far longer one than that of the Son. If we would stop to realize what heaven is and then how different this dark and sinful world must seem in comparison with that glorious abode we

19

will be able to form some idea of the infinite condescension of the Holy Spirit. Some realization of it is possible, if we look at the lives of missionaries who have gone forth from happy Christian homes and immured themselves for a whole lifetime among the brutal and degraded people of some heathen land. Far deeper was the descent of the Holy Spirit in coming from heaven to earth and dwelling for all these ages in continual contact with the selfishness, wickedness and uncleanness of this polluted world.

2. The love of the Spirit is seen in His union with the Lord Jesus Christ during His earthly ministry and His partnership with Him in all that He felt and said and did. All the Savior's works of beneficence were equally wrought by the Holy Ghost who rested upon Him; all His greatest words were spoken at the impulse and through the anointment of the Holy Spirit.

Do we admire and adore the love of Jesus in forgiving sinners, in comforting mourners, in healing sick and suffering men and women and in taking the little children in His arms? That was also the love of the Spirit. Do we love to remember His gentle and gracious promises, those immortal words of love and grace that never can be forgotten, and that no human language can ever parallel or approach? That was all spoken through the Spirit quite as much as by the lips of the Lord.

3. The love of the Spirit is seen in the grace with which He seeks and saves lost sinners. In the

three parables of Luke 15, the Holy Spirit is represented by the woman's invincible patience and perseverance as she swept the house and sought diligently till she found it; so the Holy Spirit seeks the lost jewels of human souls in the dust and grime of sin, sparing no pains and counting no time too long until at last He finds and restores them.

There are men and women in heaven today who met all the approaches of divine grace for nearly a whole lifetime with hardness of heart, indifference and even scorn, and who at last were won to God through His patient love. How we shall adore Him some day as He takes us back over our past and at every stage reminds us again, "I have loved you with an everlasting love; I have drawn you with loving-kindness" (Jeremiah 31:3).

4. The Holy Spirit's love is manifested in His indwelling in human hearts, His making our bodies His temples, and His infinite and ceaseless tenderness and care in our spiritual life and training. What condescension for the most glorious of beings to become incarnate in some poor man, some humble beggar, some illiterate convert who has just accepted Christ in the slums of one of our cities. In such lowly habitations the heavenly Comforter condescends to dwell for a lifetime, patiently teaching, cleansing and comforting. Like a true mother the Holy Spirit is always busy with His charge. Nothing is too trifling for His interest; nothing is too hard for His love and power. Truly we may say:

Like a web of loving kindness,
All our life His mercy wove,
Every thread and fibre telling,
Of His everlasting love.

5. The love of the Spirit is suggested by the language used even when we offend Him. The Scriptures do not speak of the anger, but of the grief of this gentle Friend: "Grieve not the Holy Spirit of God, whereby ye are sealed unto the day of redemption." How this ought to humble us and make us ashamed of our negligence and disobedience!

6. The Holy Spirit loves us with a jealous love. In James 4:5 we read, "The spirit he caused to live in us envies intensely." The Holy Spirit is grieved when Christians set their affections upon the world and allow anything to separate them from supreme devotion to the Lord Jesus. With such a loving Friend let us also be jealous for His supreme rights and endeavors so to live that He will find in us the satisfaction and the delight which we have found in Him.

THE ROCK AND THE RIVER

*They drank from the spiritual rock that ac-
companied them, and that rock was Christ.*
(1 Corinthians 10:4)

Among the beautiful types of spiritual truth
in the Old Testament there is none more
striking or significant than the rock in Horeb, of
which we read in Exodus 17:2–7, and again in
Numbers 20:8–12. The Rock in Horeb was a type
of Jesus Christ, the Rock of Ages. The striking of
that rock set forth the death of Jesus on the cross
under the stroke of divine judgment. And the
flowing of the waters from the rock when struck
foreshadowed the outpouring of the Holy Spirit
as a result of Christ's atoning death. The Apostle
John connects this with the piercing of His side

by the Roman soldier when he says, "This is the one who came by water and blood—Jesus Christ. He did not come by water only, but by water and blood. And it is the Spirit who testifies, because the Spirit is the truth" (1 John 5:6). The Holy Spirit therefore was poured out at Pentecost following Christ's finished work. The Comforter is closely associated with the precious blood in the Old Testament. The oil was always poured upon the blood and we cannot have the Holy Ghost apart from the cross of Jesus Christ. The water which flowed from the split rock suggests the cleansing, refreshing, satisfying influences of the blessed Comforter. He is for us the "Water of Life" so constantly referred to in the New Testament.

In the second passage referred to in Numbers we have an entirely different scene. A whole generation has passed since the rock was struck. Once more the people are famishing with thirst and once more Moses leads them at God's command to the rock. But this time the rock is not to be struck, for it has been struck once and is open still. Instead Moses is commanded to "speak to the rock," and the waters will flow forth abundantly. He is to use the language of faith and claim the blessing which is already waiting His acceptance. Instead of doing this Moses becomes excited and violently strikes the rock three times. God does not fail to respond by causing the water to flow in abundance, but He is grieved with Moses for his disobedience and haste, and consequently Moses is not allowed to enter the Land of Promise a few years later.

Now all this is full of deep spiritual teaching. This incident typifies our present relation to the Holy Spirit. Pentecost has come. The Spirit is given. The heavens are opened. The water of life is flowing. We do not have to bring the Spirit now for He is here. We have only to "speak to the Rock." That is, we are to come in simple trust and claim the fullness of the Spirit who has been given, and as we open our hearts to drink the water will flow at our bidding. There is no need for excitement or noisy demonstrations and incantations, but faith can calmly take what the Spirit is lovingly waiting to give.

> Speak to the Rock,
> Bid the waters flow,
> Doubt not the Spirit,
> Given long ago,
> Take what He waiteth
> Freely to bestow;
> Drink till thy being
> All His fullness know.

We pass on to the next chapter of Numbers and find a still more striking and beautiful illustration of the Holy Spirit in verses 16–18. Again they were suffering from thirst and no water appeared in sight. But this time they do not seek the rock, but gather in a circle in the sand and with their staves dig a well, accompanying the digging with a song of faith and invocation, "Spring up, O well! Sing about it." And as they dug and sang their song of faith the waters gushed up from subterranean fountains and they drank in abundance. The waters which had flowed from the struck rock were evidently running as a subterranean river beneath their feet, and all they had to do was to tap the river and drink abundantly and be satisfied. This is what is meant by the "Rock that accompanied them." The Rock itself did not move, but the waters that flowed from it followed them all through the wilderness.

How full of simple and glorious meaning is this little picture! We may not always see the river of God's fullness flowing in our lives, nor be distinctly conscious of the Spirit's gracious presence. Often we shall be entirely without religious feeling or emotion, but the Holy Spirit is still there in the depths of our subconscious being. In the moment of need we can, like them, dig a well of faith and prayer, and best of all by song and praise, and then the fountains will gush forth, the living waters will flow, and our happy hearts will sing, "There is a river whose streams make glad the city of God" (Psalm 46:4a).

THE WELLSPRING
AND THE RIVER

The water I give him will become in him a
spring of water, welling up to eternal life.
(John 4:14)
Whoever believes in me, as the Scripture
has said, streams of living water will flow
from within him. (John 7:38)

We miss the meaning of this first passage if we forget the difference between a well and a wellspring. The Lord is speaking of an artesian well that flows from hidden fountains and gushes up in perennial freshness and fullness. This is the Lord's own figure of ideal spiritual life and of the results of the indwelling of the Comforter. This is not trying to be good and slowly and painfully building up character by ethical culture; but this is a spontaneous life that flows from sources beyond ourselves and that works automatically, uniformly and effectually in spite of all conditions, hindrances and even natural tendencies. This is the promise of that glorious gospel in Ezekiel which so fully anticipated the advanced revelation of the New Testament, "And I will put My Spirit in you and move you to follow my decrees, and be careful to keep my laws" (36:27). This is the law of spiritual life in Christ Jesus, the new law of gravitation which the apostle says "set me free from the law of sin and death" (Romans 8:26). It is a mightier force within us overcoming the tendencies of our sinful nature and making it natural for us through a new divine nature to do the things which once we hated, and avoid the things which once we loved.

It is impossible for us to analyze, dissect or trace by any biological and psychological process the method of this divine mystery. This is all we can distinctly formulate—somewhere down in the depths of our subconscious being God through the Holy Spirit takes up His abode.

His actual personal presence is hidden from our consciousness, just as the hidden spring of that artesian well is far out of sight in the bowels of the earth. All we are conscious of is the manifestation of His presence from time to time in various influences, operations, emotions and effects in our spirit and life. The Holy Spirit is just as truly in us when He makes no sign as when the fountains of joy are overflowing, or the waters of peace are softly refreshing our weary and troubled hearts.

The possibilities of the indwelling Spirit are limitless and infinitely varied. He may bring some new grace or gift into prominence in our life and work at different times as may seem best to His sovereign will. But we are not, therefore, to say that our old experience is void and that we have received a new baptism of the Spirit. It is the same blessed wellspring flowering in new streams and springing up in new fullness as it will continue to spring up "into everlasting life."

Do you know this indwelling Spirit and this heavenly wellspring? Has God taken up His abode within your heart? Can you say,

> He never is so distant from us,
> As even to be near?
> He dwells within the yielded spirit
> And makes our heaven here.

But in the seventh chapter of John our Lord passes on to a much larger truth. The wellspring has now become a river, nay, not one river only, but a mighty delta of many outflowing streams, for "streams of living water will flow from within him." The secret of this is that the direction has been changed. The river is flowing out, not in. We have been saved from the life of self and entered into the life of love, which is always the life of God.

Modern sociology calls this altruism and tries to

cultivate it on mere ethical lines of human endeavor. You can no more do this than make an artesian well by pouring water into the pump and then pumping it out as the farmers do when the well begins to run dry. No, we must be filled with the Spirit first and then the overflow will take care of itself.

But we must not fail to expect a direct overflow. This is God's test of character discipleship. "This is to my Father's glory, that you bear much fruit, showing yourselves to be my disciples" (John 15:8). Alas for the Christians that are always receiving and never giving, always seeking blessings and never being a blessing. When Mr. Moody was first in England his attention was called to a lady with an illuminated face and always listening with marked attention in one of the front seats of the auditorium. Mr Moody asked one day who she was. "Oh," said one of the committee, "we call her a bog. She has attended every religious service within her reach for years, and is always after a blessing, but no one ever knew her to do anything to help another soul, either by her hands, her testimony, or her purse. And so we call her a bog, which you know is a waterhole that never discharges its stagnant water." Are you a bog or an artesian well and a river of living water?

THE RIVER FROM THE SANCTUARY

. . . and I saw water coming out from
under the threshold of the temple . . .
(Ezekiel 47:1)

While Ezekiel's magnificent vision of the river from the sanctuary will have no doubt a literal fulfillment some future day, yet it is part of that great flood of sacred symbolism which has flowed down through the course of divine revelation from the rivers of Eden to the river of the water of life flowing from the throne of God and the Lamb. The most direct significance of this living stream is ever the Holy Spirit applying to us the blessings of Christ's redeeming work.

The first thing we notice about Ezekiel's river is

its apparent insignificance. The word translated "coming out" literally means "trickled." Just a few tiny drops were trickling down the little channel and it scarcely could be called a river. The first manifestations of the Holy Spirit are often faint and almost imperceptible; but the touch of God's little finger always means that God Himself is behind even the slightest manifestations of His presence and His working. Let us cherish the first faint touches of spiritual life and divine grace and soon we will "press on to acknowledge him" (Hosea 6:3a).

The river broadens and deepens as it flows and after the first measurement it has become a considerable stream so that it is described as "water that was ankle-deep." The spiritual significance of the figure now becomes apparent and important. "Water that was ankle-deep" suggests walking in the Spirit, practical obedience to the heavenly voice and the inward presence. The first distinct manifestation of the Spirit will usually come in connection with our doing something at God's command, or yielding something which He has forbidden. The Holy Spirit is "given to those who obey Him." God comes to us with a touch of blessing, and then He tests our loyalty by requiring some act of surrender or obedience and as we step in obedient faith into the flood we find the waters have reached our ankles and the Holy Spirit has become a practical reality in our life. Perhaps, dear friend, if you have not had a satisfactory experience of the Comforter, it is because

He is waiting for you to follow His leading in some first step of obedience that you have not yet taken. If you wait upon Him with an honest purpose He will not fail to show you what is hindering His further blessing.

But the river still moves on and the next measurement finds "water that was knee-deep." Surely this is not hard to interpret. We shall not have traveled far with the Comforter before we have begun to learn the holy mystery of prayer, the prayer of the Holy Spirit.

This is very different from our own conventional or ordinary prayers. This is "the oracle of the Lord," the voice of One that "intercedes for us with groans that words cannot express." A supernatural pressure, sometimes of deep sadness and keen suffering, will drive us to our knees, and as we pour out our hearts and roll over our burden, there will come to us such a sense of God's response that we will know that we are praying in the Holy Ghost and it will be "water that is knee-deep."

Still the river flows onward and downward, and now it is "water that was up to the waist [loins]." The loins always stand for the seat of life and power. The girded loins mean strength, energy, power. Water to the loins therefore signifies the spirit of "power when the Holy Spirit comes on you; and you will be my witnesses" (Acts 1:8b). Beloved, do you know anything of this divine enabling for the winning of souls, for the help of tried ones, for the prayer of faith, for the Spirit of revival and the success and progress of the kingdom of God?

The last measurement of this mighty river brings us to the end of all fathoming and measuring lines. We have got clear beyond our depth. It is "water to swim in, a river that no one could cross." Surely this is the fullness of the Holy Ghost, a life so lost in God that we cease to recognize ourselves in the mightier Presence that overshadows us and carries us by a divine impulse in a glorious and spontaneous life. When we reach this stage we think little of our own feelings and experiences and are absorbed in the Lord Jesus and the life divine. Speaking of Himself Paul could say "I know a man in Christ." He has ceased to be himself in the old sense and had become "a man in Christ."

> There the Lord will be our Mighty One.
>   It will be like a place of broad rivers and
>   streams.
> No galley with oars will ride them,
>   No mighty ship will sail them.
>   (Isaiah 33:21)

"No galley with oars will ride them" for the good reason that the current carries us and we do not need to paddle any more.

Then follow the fruits of the Spirit, the trees upon the bank of this mighty river, with leaves unfading and fruit ripening every month and leaves also "for healing," "so where the river flows everything will live" (Ezekiel 47:9b); while beneath the flood are multitudes of fishes, and on the banks the fishermen spread their nets—all telling of the precious souls that will rejoice our hearts and fill the heavens with praise when we shall have come into the fullness of the river from the sanctuary.

THE ANOINTING
OF THE
COMFORTER

*Now it is God which makes both us and you
stand firm in Christ. He anointed us.*
(2 Corinthians 1:21)

Among the emblems of the Old Testament
there is none which is more frequently
used to set forth the office of the Holy Ghost
than the anointing oil.

The first thing we notice about it is that the oil
was always placed upon the blood. "Do not pour
it on men's bodies" was one of God's most
solemn sanctions. The carnal heart cannot receive
the Holy Spirit. Only after we have been touched
with the blood and brought into fellowship with

the death and resurrection of Jesus can we receive the Spirit in our new nature. The Holy Ghost is always associated with the cross and the precious blood.

The next typical fact which we notice is the anointing of the Tabernacle of which we have a detailed account in the last chapter of Exodus. After Moses had completed the sanctuary according to all of God's specifications, it was solemnly anointed and given over to the Lord. God immediately took possession of it and the cloud, which hitherto had hovered above it or marched before, descended and entered the Tabernacle and henceforth appeared as the Shekinah glory in the Holy of Holies.

From this time forth we find God speaking to His people not from the cloud but from within the Tabernacle. He had changed His dwelling place and was now in the midst of Israel. So important was this fact that it marked a new era in the history of the chosen people; we are particularly told that it was the beginning of the second year of their journeys in the wilderness. How it reminds us that the coming of the Holy Spirit to a human heart is the second great epoch of our spiritual life and marks a crisis just as distinct as conversion itself.

Have you entered upon the second year of your spiritual history by receiving the anointing of the Holy Ghost?

We next read in connection with the healing of the leper in the 14th chapter of Leviticus of a remarkable application of the oil, along with the blood, to the ear, the thumb and the great toe of the leper who is to be cleansed. This represents the consecration to God and the quickening by the Holy Spirit, first of all our receptive powers represented by the ear, next of all our active powers represented by the hand and finally of our life and walk represented by the foot. Have you given your ears to the Holy Ghost to hear and understand only what He would teach and speak? Have you yielded your hands to minister to God through His grace and to be wholly controlled by His power? And have you yielded your feet to walk in the Spirit and be guided wholly according to His perfect will?

The anointing oil was poured upon prophets, priests and kings to set them apart to their sacred ministry and to signify their enduement with the wisdom, holiness and power which they required for their sacred functions. So the Holy Spirit alone can call us to Christian service and fit us for it. "If anyone serves, he should do it with the strength God provides" (1 Peter 4:11a). He uses our natural powers, but in such dependence upon Him that, as the apostle expresses it in the passage already quoted, "That in all things God may be praised through Jesus Christ."

The anointing of the sick which we find our Lord commanding and the Apostle James confirming was a direct means of physical healing and was intended to set forth the quickening ministry of the Holy Spirit in the human body. All life and energy are allied to spiritual forces. The very power that moves the world and the mightiest physical force, the law of gravitation, is ethereal more than material. Physical life is an invisible and intangible force. When the Spirit moved upon Samson of old he had the strength of a hundred giants. And when the Spirit was withdrawn he was weak as a child. The Comforter, therefore, is the real source of physical life and healing and quickens the mortal bodies of those in whom He dwells.

These are but some of the blessed results of the anointing of the Holy Ghost. Surely they may well encourage us to ask how may we receive this blessed touch of divine life, power and healing. What is the anointing of the Holy Ghost? Where can we find a better answer than by turning to the example of our great Forerunner, who "had to be made like his brothers in every way . . ."? We are told that "God anointed Jesus of Nazareth with the Holy Spirit and power" (Acts 10:38). We know when that occurred. It was not in His childhood, although He had been born through the agency of the Holy Spirit and during His childhood and youth walked with God and under the direction of the Holy Spirit. But it marked a distinct crisis in His life when, after yielding Himself to His Father's will and His appointed work, He received direct visitation of the Holy Spirit who henceforth abode upon Him and became the source of all His strength and ministry. For us His disciples also there is the same definite second experience of the anointing of the Holy Ghost if we will meet the conditions like Him. Beloved, "Did you receive the Holy Spirit when you believed" (Acts 19:2a)?

Tenth Day

BAPTIZED
WITH FIRE

*He will baptize you with the Holy Spirit
and with fire.* (Matthew 3:11)

The mightiest physical force we know is fire. Hence from the earliest ages, even in false religions, it has been recognized as a symbol of the supernatural and even worshiped and deified. It is one of the oldest divine emblems of the Holy Ghost. We see it in the flaming sword at the gates of Eden, the burning lamps that appeared to Abraham in connection with his sacrifice, the burning bush in which God appeared to Moses in the land of Midian, the pillar of cloud and fire which led the Israelites, the consuming fire that enshrouded Mount Sinai, the Shekinah glory in the Holy of Holies, the fire that answered Elijah's prayer and settled the test of the false and true God in Israel, and many other illustrations closing with the Pentecostal flame which marked the advent of the Holy Ghost.

We should first notice that the baptism of fire is not different from the baptism with the Holy Ghost. It is simply an expletive phrase qualifying and completing the thought expressed in the first phrase. The Holy Ghost is Himself a Divine Fire, and when He takes possession of a soul His operations are similar to the effect of fire in the natural world. The baptism with fire, however, suggests a stronger and more searching operation of the Spirit than that which is expressed by the other figure of water which John employs. Even in the Old Testament types and ceremonials we find God making a distinction between water and fire, especially in one striking passage where it was commanded that everything must be purified either by water or fire, and that if it could not stand fire it was to be purified by water. Does this imply that God deals differently with different souls according to their spiritual capacity and the completeness of their surrender to Him? Is it because you are not able or willing to stand the fire that you have not received it and God has had to deal with you in a less thorough and searching way?

We have a reference to the purifying effects of fire in Malachi 3:2: "He will be like a refiner's fire or a launderer's soap. He will sit as a refiner and purifier of silver; he will purify the Levites."

Malachi is speaking of the work of the jeweler as he sits before his crucible watching the fierce flame as it eliminates the dross and leaves the silver so perfectly refined that at length He can see his face in the glowing metal. So the Holy Spirit sits down in His slow and patient work in a surrendered heart, revealing and removing selfishness and sin until at last the image of Christ shines from all our inner being.

We have a very solemn picture of the testing fire in First Corinthians 3:13: "The fire will test the quality of each man's work." While this undoubtedly refers to the testing fires of the final day, yet the language of John the Baptist distinctly implies that every one of us must pass through one of two fires. We must either have the purifying fire of the Holy Spirit now or that later flame of which He says, "[burns] up the chaff with unquenchable fire" (Matthew 3:12b).

"Our God is a consuming fire" (Hebrews 12:29), is not wholly an angry threat. Rather it is a revelation of God in His sanctifying grace and power. It is "our God" who is a "consuming fire." There are things in all of us that we are not able to eliminate ourselves, and we would give any price to have consumed. It is such a privilege to have a fire on which we can lay them through our great Sin Offering and to have them burn to ashes outside the camp. Beloved, have you experienced the blessedness of having God's fire burn out your inmost being? Do you know what it is to lay over everything of the flesh and self and sin on the Lamb of God as your Sin Offering, and then see Him consumed with your sin outside the camp while your soul is cleansed and emancipated and you joyfully sing:

> Oh fire of God, burn on, burn on,
> Till all my dross is burned away;
> Oh, fire of God, burn on, burn on,
> Prepare me for the testing day.

The Holy Ghost kindles in the soul the fires of love, the flame that melts our selfishness and pours out our being in tenderness, sacrifice and service. And the same fire of love is the fusing, uniting flame, which makes Christians one, even as the volcanic tide that rolls down the mountain fuses into one current everything in its course.

Above all things fire is the mightiest of forces. It drives our engines and propels our commerce. It is the only thing that can move the heart of man and the Church of God. Oh, for the dynamite of the Holy Ghost:

> Oh, for a passionate passion for souls,
> Oh, for the pity that yearns!
> Oh, for the love that loves unto death,
> Oh, for the fire that burns!

THE BREAST
OF GOD

*And with that he breathed on them and
said, "Receive the Holy Spirit."*
(John 20:22)

The air we breathe is one of the most refined
and yet most necessary and powerful of all
the elements of nature. We have learned through
the progress of modern science that it is as
material and substantial as the ground upon
which we tread, or the rocks and solid mountain,
although in a much finer and fluid state. It can be
compressed into liquid form until it becomes
more powerful than dynamite. It contributes
much of the life of plants and animals and as the
enveloping atmosphere of our globe radiates to us
the solar heat and light and forms a curtain of

45

defense between us and innumerable perils from the countless fragments of disrupted worlds that are ever floating around us in space. It lends itself with great propriety and forcefulness to the illustration of spiritual truth and it is one of the most striking symbols of the Holy Spirit.

This is implied in the symbolic act of the Lord Jesus in connection with our text, when "He breathed on them," or perhaps breathed before them, and said, "Receive the Holy Spirit." The latter interpretation has in it a very impressive suggestion. By the act of exhaling and inhaling the air through His lungs He gave them an object lesson of the way in which we may receive the Holy Ghost. Breathing out our old natural life with one exhalation, and breathing in the new spiritual life from the Holy Spirit with the next inhalation. This really expresses the highest attitude of the abiding life.

> I am breathing every moment,
> Drawing all my life from Thee.
> Breath by breath I live upon Thee,
> Blessed Spirit, breathe in me.
> I am breathing out my own life
> That I may be filled with Thine,
> Letting go my strength and weakness,
> Breathing in Thy strength divine.

The other interpretation of this beautiful text links our spiritual life and our spiritual anointing most intimately with the Lord Jesus Himself. The

Holy Spirit is the Spirit of Jesus and by this symbolic act He transferred His very Spirit to the disciples and passed over His vital breath into their
being. Thus He identified the Spirit with Himself
as well as Himself with them. And thus He taught
us as well as them that we are never to try to
receive the Holy Spirit apart from Jesus, but by
fellowship with Jesus and by breathing in His
own very life. Jesus is the One that baptizes with
the Holy Ghost, and while this is true in the first
bestowing of the Spirit, it is also true in every
successive infilling of His blessed presence. How
exquisitely the figure suggests such intimacy with
our blessed Savior that we receive the very kiss of
His lips and the very breath of His being.

The same figure is used in many other references to the Holy Spirit. The Pentecostal outpouring was accompanied by the "sound like the
blowing of a violent wind from heaven" (Acts
2:2b). How tremendous is the power wrapped up
in the winds of heaven! What more forcible figure could be employed to denote the resistless
energy of the almighty Spirit! The same figure
was also employed by the Prophet Ezekiel in the
Vision of the Dry Bones, where he summons the
Spirit to "Come from the four winds, O breath,
and breathe into these slain, that they may live"
(37:9b). The representation here is the Spirit of
Life as the mighty breath of God. We are carried
back still farther by the figure to the morning of
creation when "the Lord God . . . breathed into
his nostrils the breath of life and the man became

a living being" (Genesis 2:7b). Our breath is so identified with our life that when we cease to breathe we cease to live. But our life did not come to us in the first instance as a mere animal impulse, but from the very breath of the Creator. And so our spiritual life is as directly supernatural and divine. Ezekiel's prophesying could bring about the physical reconstruction of the forms of men, but there was no life in them. It was when the Spirit came from the four winds that they rose up and stood upon their feet an exceeding great army. Man's teaching and preaching can produce certain social and ethical transformations but cannot give true spiritual life. There are lots of churches like Ezekiel's dry bones after they were reconstructed, or Coleridge's Dream of the Ancient Mariner; but there is a dead man in the pulpit and there are only dead men and women in the pews.

Our Lord refers in the third chapter of John to the agency of the Holy Spirit in the new birth under the figure of the air or wind. "The wind blows where it pleases. You can hear its sound, but you cannot tell where it comes from or where it is going. So it is with everyone born of the Spirit" (8). The operations of the Comforter, like the wind, are mysterious and hidden. We know them by their effects. We cannot trace the working of His hands but we can see and feel the purity, the peace, the joy, the love and the fruits of blessing on every hand that follow that working.

Twelfth Day

THE SEALING OF THE HOLY GHOST

*Having believed, you were marked in him
with a seal, the promised Holy Spirit.*
(Ephesians 1:13b)

The use of a seal in human business contracts and legal transactions is as old as human society.

The first thing suggested by a seal is reality. The seal leaves a definite, visible and tangible mark that no one can mistake. So the Holy Spirit makes Christian experience actual, real and conscious. That which we have taken by simple faith now becomes a matter of living experience. This is what was meant when the Apostle John said, "The law was given through Moses; grace and truth [reality] came through Jesus Christ" (John

1:17). The law was only a "shadow of the good things that are coming" (Hebrews 10:1a), a promise and a type of things that had not yet materialized. Jesus Christ brings to us, by the Holy Spirit, the very substance of those things. When the sinner believes in the Lord Jesus Christ his first step is to take by simple faith the promise of forgiveness and full salvation, and then to reckon upon God's Word and count the things that are not as though they were. But, after faith is tested and proved, the Holy Spirit brings to the heart the conscious witness of all that we have believed for, and sheds abroad the peace, love and joy of the Lord in our happy hearts, and we can say now, "I know whom I have believed" (2 Timothy 1:12b). So, in all other experiences of faith, there is the two-fold stage, first of believing and reckoning, and then of realizing and knowing.

The Scriptures themselves speak of two seals in this connection. First, there is our seal which faith places upon God's promise when it takes Him at His Word and counts Him true. "The man who has accepted it has certified [set his seal, KJV] that God is truthful" (John 3:33). When we really believe God we commit ourselves to His Word as completely as when the notary puts his stamp upon a business contract. But now having set our seal to the promise, God comes and adds His seal upon ours. "Having believed, you were marked in him with a seal, the promised Holy Spirit" (Ephesians 1:13b). God makes real to our spiritual senses that which we accepted, without feeling, in naked faith, and now we know as well as believe. Hence the Apostle John declares, "Anyone who believes in the Son of God has this testimony in his heart" (1 John 5:10). We have no right to look for the witness or for any inward sense of divine acceptance until after we have first believed without it, and then God will surely give it.

It is all right, therefore, to tell people not to wait for feeling, but simply to take God at His Word. But there is a limit to this. After we have taken God at His Word there is a place for feeling, experience and all the fruits of the Spirit, which are love, joy, peace and a long catalog of other spiritual experiences. Beloved friend, have you set your seal to God's Word, first for your salvation and then for every other blessing that you have a right to claim for spirit, soul and body? And have you also claimed and obtained the Holy Spirit's sealing and realizing touch, so that you can say with the apostle, "You are the Christ, the Son of the living God" (Matthew 16:16)? "We know also that the Son of God has come and has given us understanding, so that we may know Him who is true. And we are in Him who is true—even in His Son Jesus Christ" (1 John 5:20).

The second meaning of a seal is security, certainty and the guarantee of all contained in the paper sealed. The seal accredits the document and gives assurance that all the contracts will be fulfilled. And so the Holy Spirit as God's Seal gives to the heart full assurance of faith and the absolute certainty that we shall inherit all His covenant promises. There is undoubtedly a place into which the believer may come where doubt and fear have forever passed away and the spirit rests upon the "strong consolation" not only of God's promise, but of God's oath, as "an anchor of the soul, firm and secure. It enters the inner sanctuary behind the curtain" (Hebrews 6:19). Henceforth its attitude is, "I know whom I have believed, and am convinced that He is able to guard what I have entrusted to Him for that day" (2 Timothy 1:12). This blessed experience is the result of full committal, entire consecration and, in consequence, the sealing of the Holy Ghost. Speaking of such an experience the Apostle Peter says, "Be all the more eager to make your calling and election sure. For if you do these things, you will never fall, and you will receive a rich welcome into the eternal kingdom of our Lord and Savior Jesus Christ" (2 Peter 1:10–11).

Once more, the seal implies resemblance. It transmits its own image to the sensitive wax or the written page. It leaves a copy of its own face upon the object sealed. And so the Holy Spirit when He seals us not only makes the Lord Jesus real to our consciousness, but also the pattern and the very substance of our Christian character. He so unites us with Him that henceforth Jesus Himself lives in us, conforming us to His holy image and transforming and transfiguring us "into his likeness with ever-increasing glory, which comes from the Lord, who is the Spirit" (2 Corinthians 3:18b).

Thirteenth Day

THE DYNAMITE OF GOD

*But you will receive power (dynamite)
when the Holy Spirit comes on you, and you
will be my witnesses.* (Acts 1:8)

Our word "dynamite," which represents one
of the most powerful substances known to
modern science, is derived and practically transferred with scarcely a change of sound or spelling,
from the Greek word used for "power" in this
and many other texts in the New Testament. The
Holy Spirit is the mightiest dynamic force of the
spiritual world. Indeed, He is the One supreme
spiritual Force, and He is promised to the
believer and the Church as the Source of their
spiritual power.

There is nothing we need more than power.

Man, once the lord of nature, is now one of the weakest of all earthly beings. The human babe is more helpless than the infant progeny of any living creature, and often requires almost a quarter of a lifetime to grow strong enough to be able to take care of himself. Your little child is feebler than the tiger's cub, and you yourself are impotent before the lightning, the wind, the flame, the plague, and the wild beasts of the wilderness. Still more weak is man, morally and spiritually. His own nature is hopelessly broken down by the love and power of sin; his own tendencies are wrong; and spiritual forces of evil around him on every side tend to draw him away from the path of right and safety.

The salvation of the Lord Jesus Christ, therefore, comes to us with the promise of divine power, and the instrument of this power is the Holy Spirit.

The power which the Holy Spirit brings to us is first of all power to be, and then power to do and suffer. Our personal character and our moral and spiritual victories are of more importance than our testimony and work. No man can successfully lead others to a higher plane of Christian living who is not himself overcoming temptation and living a pure and heavenly life. Even Gibbon, the infidel historian, confessed that the chief secret of the earthly triumph of Christianity was the pure and victorious lives of the early Christians. There is no argument against a good life. Our first need, therefore, is power to overcome sin and manifest the virtues and attractions of goodness, love, patience, and self-sacrifice.

The power of the Holy Spirit is also specially manifest in inspiring us with Christian fortitude and strengthening us "so that you may have great endurance and patience, and joyfully giving thanks to the Father . . ." (Colossians 1:11b–12a). To be able to endure injustice, reproach and wrong without resentment and even with sweetness and benignity is not a human virtue and requires the very power of God in the Christian. The mightiest triumphs of the Holy Spirit's power are still found along these lines of passive endurance and patient suffering.

I remember a quiet, practical woman who a few years ago, in a special religious meeting, received the baptism of the Holy Spirit. The change in her life that followed was not one marked by any great public demonstration or active ministry, but it made her a better wife and mother and a sweeter influence in her large home circle. At last there came to her the greatest of earthly trials and I was summoned to visit her as a broken hearted widow, suddenly bereaved of the husband and companion of 50 happy years.

I expected to find her in the depths of sorrow. Instead she met me with a beaming and triumphant face and as she clasped my hand she asked, "Am I wrong to be so happy? My children tell me that I should be weeping like them, but my heart is so full of the joy of the Lord that I cannot shed a tear." The Comforter had come and the power of God had carried her above the waves of sorrow.

But the power of the Spirit is given to us, finally, not only to be and suffer, but to do. There is work for us to accomplish for the Master and the world. There are words to be spoken in His name. There are souls to be sought and won. There are lives to be transformed and consecrated to His service. There is only One who can give us "power with God and with men" (Genesis 32:28b, KJV), the blessed Holy Spirit. It is His province to kindle our hearts with love, to inspire our souls with faith, to clothe our words with holy unction, so that men will not hear us, but Him; will not see us, but their own sinfulness and the Savior's grace; will not praise us but will turn to God and "produce fruit in keeping with repentance" (Matthew 3:8). "He will convict the world of guilt in regard to sin and righteousness and judgment" (John 16:8). We may interest the world, we may attract the world, but He only can convict the world. The ministry needed to-day is a ministry of spiritual power.

The Lord Jesus did not attempt to begin His ministry until He had received this power. Have you been "clothed with power from on high"?

Fourteenth Day

THE HOLY SPIRIT AN EARNEST

Who is a deposit [earnest] guaranteeing our
inheritance until the redemption of those
who are God's possession.
(Ephesians 1:14)

The word "earnest" was used in ancient times
in connection with legal forms and business
transactions. When a piece of real estate was purchased it was customary for the seller to give to
the purchaser a little bag or handful of the very
soil which he had bought as a pledge that in due
time the whole of the estate would likewise be
transferred and the sale complete. This is still the
usage in China and some other Oriental countries
today. And I once had the opportunity of receiving such a little bag of sand from a Chinese attor-

ney in connection with the purchase of mission property in that country.

The use of this figure in connection with the Holy Spirit represents the Spirit in His present indwelling in our hearts and His gracious influences upon us as being the guarantee and pledge of all the blessings of redemption that are still awaiting us in the coming ages. The Spirit brings to us part of our inheritance now as the assurance that all the rest will follow in due time. The earnest was not only similar, but identical. It was the very soil of the estate purchased. And so the Holy Spirit gives to us the very substance of all the blessings of salvation which are yet awaiting us.

The joy of heaven is our eternal inheritance, but the Holy Spirit gives us in this present time a foretaste of eternal joy. Perfect purity and likeness to God will constitute part of the glory of our future life. But the Holy Spirit sanctified us here and gives us the blessed foretaste of heaven.

Our final salvation is to involve a higher physical life and our bodies are to be raised up at the coming of our Lord in strength, immortality and glory, and to share His own perfect, boundless and incorruptible life for ever more. But the Holy Spirit has not left us without the physical earnest of the coming resurrection in the healing of our bodies from pain and sickness through simple faith in the name of Jesus, in the quickening life which He imparts to all our mortal frame when we fully trust and touch Him. We have even here the first pulses of the coming resurrection and the earnest of immortality and glory. Divine healing is just a little heart-throb of resurrection life coming in advance of the advent. And it is our privilege to draw upon our future heritage in this respect and know even here a little of the joy and glory of the resurrection morning. In the fifth chapter of Second Corinthians the apostle dwells particularly upon this somewhat obscure truth, teaching us that we have now the elements of our future tabernacle. And he adds, "Now it is God who has made us for this very purpose and has given us the Spirit as a deposit [earnest], guaranteeing what is to come" (5:5). The same truth is taught by Paul in the eighth chapter of Romans where he says, "We ourselves, who have the first fruits of the Spirit, groan inwardly as we wait eagerly for our adoption as sons, the redemption of our bodies" (8:23).

Again, the future life will bring us an exalted condition of all the powers of our intellectual being. "Then I shall know fully, as I am fully known" (1 Corinthians 13:12b), and all our faculties will expand into the complete likeness of His glory. But the Spirit is the earnest of even this in our present life. "We have the mind of Christ" (1 Corinthians 2:16b), as well as His physical quickening in our body. Every power of our intellect may be enlarged by the Spirit's quickening life.

The coming age is to bring the world's restoration. Physically, socially and politically the curse of sin will be destroyed and a constitution of liberty, peace and happiness will be universal. All

the powers of nature will be completely controlled by the mind of man and made subservient to
the welfare and happiness of human society. This
old storm-tossed earth, torn with earthquake and
volcano and transformed into a very sepulcher
will become the abode of universal life and joy
and "the desert and the parched land will be
glad;/ the wilderness will rejoice and blossom"
(Isaiah 35:1a). But even of this God is giving the
earnest in our time. The discoveries of science,
the marvelous progress of human knowledge, in-
vention, refinement and culture are all
foreshadowings of that coming age when man
will be by God's complete approval the Lord of
nature and the vicegerent of heaven on earth
below. Just as the winter leaves which the
botanists may find hidden beneath the hard,
protecting buds and husks of December, contain
wrapped in the bosom of these rough shells the
soft and living germs of next summer's foliage
and blossoms, so even in this old wintry world we
can trace already the harbingers of the coming
spring and the earnest of the new creation. God's
chosen Israel is scattered over all the earth, and
the promise of Zion's future glory seems like an
empty dream. But even amid all this wreck and
apostasy God is gathering out a people from the
chosen race, while from the Gentiles He is
gathering out a people for His name, and in
countless signals we can already trace the earnest
of the Lord's return and the millennial age of
peace and glory.

THE SPIRIT OF HOLINESS

You were sanctified . . . by the Spirit of our God. (1 Corinthians 6:11)

The Holy Spirit is the Sanctifier. Next to conversion His greatest work is to deliver from the power of sin and restore to the image of Christ.

He does this by producing in the believer the spirit of conviction for cleansing. This is different from conviction of sin as it precedes justification. Then the soul is chiefly concerned about its acts of sin and the danger of sin's dread penalty. But now the Holy Spirit opens our eyes to see our innate sinfulness. He reveals the law in all its length and breadth and searches the heart in all its hidden depths, until, like Job, we cry: "Now my eyes have seen you./ Therefore I despise myself/ and repent in dust and ashes" (42:5b–6).

Sometimes in this experience the soul becomes utterly discouraged and even questions the genuineness of the former work of conversion. But it is just because of God's inexorable love to us that He presses us on the full realization of our utter corruption and helplessness. It is as when the miner discovers or buys a piece of precious ore. He has bought it and it is of priceless value in his eyes. But there is another process through which it must go. It must be crushed to powder. It must pass through the separating floods which wash away the sand and leave the gold. It must go through the fiery crucible until all the dross is separated. We can imagine the ore protesting against all this violence, but the owner might well reply, "It is because you are so precious that you must suffer all these pains in the process of purification." And so the Holy Spirit witnesses to the heart under the searching fires of His cleansing the sweet message of His love, and the trusting soul can answer back, "When He has tested me I will come forth as gold."

We have a fine illustration of this work of the Spirit in the seventh chapter of Romans, where the apostle describes a man immediately after his conversion. "Once I was alive apart from law but when the commandment came, sin sprang to life and I died" (9). He felt very much alive in the joy of salvation and perhaps imagined that he should never want to sin any more. We have all felt like this. But when the Holy Spirit began to search him through the law, he found the flesh resisting and rebelling and leading him back into former sin and his hope died and for a little he gave up even the assurance of salvation. God has to let us fight this fight alone in order to find out that we are unequal to it. At last he gave up with a cry of despair, "What a wretched man I am! Who will rescue me from this body of death?" (24). It was then that the revelation came to him through the blessed Holy Spirit of God's divine method of sanctification.

This leads us immediately to the next stage of the Spirit's sanctifying work, which we find in the succeeding chapter of Romans, the eighth. The principle of divine holiness has never been better stated than in the second verse of this chapter, "Because through Christ Jesus the law of the spirit of life set me free from the law of sin and death." Here are two laws, the old law of sin and death bearing us down and stronger than our power of resistance. It is like the law of gravitation that allows an object to fall when I drop it from my hand. But when I put forth my hand and lift it up I overcome the law of gravitation by the stronger law of life. This is exactly what the Holy Spirit does when He sanctifies us. He puts into us the new law of life by putting Christ Himself into us as our life and the old law of sin and death is overcome and the soul rises by a new law of gravitation to its heavenly sphere in the life and love and will of God. The Holy Spirit is represented in this passage as doing this, and yet He does not do it apart from Christ. He does it as "the Spirit of life in Christ Jesus." And so it is true on the one hand that we are sanctified by the Holy Ghost; and yet it is just as true on the other that "Christ Jesus, who has become for us wisdom from God—that is, our righteousness, holiness and redemption" (1 Corinthians 11:30).

The following verses of the eighth chapter of Romans unfold the successive stages of the Holy Spirit's work in our deeper life. The Spirit is represented as leading us. We "live according to the Spirit" (4). We "have our minds set on what the Spirit desires" (5). "The mind controlled by the Spirit is life and peace" (6). "Those who are led by the Spirit of God are sons of God" (14).

In this connection we must not overlook the place of the Word as used by the Spirit in our sanctification. "Sanctify them by the truth; your Word is truth" (John 17:17). And so we read of Christ sanctifying the church, "cleansing her by the washing with water through the word" (Ephesians 5:26). The Comforter brings to our remembrance the Word of God as the apostle expresses it, "for teaching, rebuking, correcting and training in righteousness, so that the man of God may be thoroughly equipped for every good work" (2 Timothy 3:16–17).

There is, therefore, at once an instantaneous and also a progressive experience of sanctification and it is the province of the blessed Comforter to give us both.

THE QUICKENING SPIRIT

And if the Spirit of Him who raised Jesus from the dead is living in you, He who raised Christ from the dead will also give life to [quicken] your mortal bodies through His Spirit who lives in you. (Romans 8:11)

This text reveals the Comforter as the Quickener or Author of life. The verse depends for its force upon the place we give it in the plan of redemption and the true exegesis of the passage. It has been usual to refer it to the future resurrection and to the work of the Holy Spirit in calling to immortal life the dead bodies of the saints of God. But there are the strongest reasons in the passage itself and the analogy of Scripture against this view.

In the first place the Holy Spirit is not represented in the Scriptures as the Agent in the final resurrection. It is the Lord Jesus who shall raise the dead by His own direct voice. "The dead will hear the voice of the Son of God and those who hear will live" (John 8:25b).

In the next place the Spirit is represented as now dwelling in the body that He quickens. This could not be true of the dead. The Holy Spirit is never represented as dwelling in a dead body. "He is not the God of the dead, but of the living" (Matthw 22:32b). It must therefore be the bodies of living persons that the Holy Spirit is here said to quicken.

Further, the bodies here quickened are described as "mortal bodies." Now a mortal body is not a dead body, but a body liable to death.

Once more, the word "quicken" does not necessarily mean the resurrection of the dead body. In this very book of Romans it is applied to the quickening of Abraham's body (4:17), when he was old and his strength was renewed for the birth of Isaac. It means the invigorating, vitalizing, stimulating of a body weak and failing, and precisely applies to the healing of disease by the touch of the Holy Spirit.

And this appears to be the obvious meaning of the passage. The apostle has just been speaking of the work of the Holy Ghost in sanctifying the soul and directing and controlling the believer's walk and life. Naturally, therefore, he next refers to the Holy Spirit's work for the Christian's body and tells us that He who is a new and divine law of life for the soul is just as much the Quickener of the weak and mortal body. If He dwells in the house He will repair it and take good care of it. Later in the chapter the writer comes to the resurrection and the future life and speaks fully of it.

The writer has fully discussed the spiritual working of the Holy Ghost in the previous paragraph and in perfect logical order is now dealing with the body, which naturally follows. We are thus introduced to God's great secret of true physical life. It is not nerve force, muscular force, the effect of food and air and constitution, although all these have their place and none of them must be neglected or despised; but it is a direct infusion into our mortal frame and our vital centers of supernatural and divine vitality through the Holy Ghost. It is something not communicated by drugs or electrical applications, or even air and food, but it is life from the primal source of life, the Creator Himself. It is another kind of life, a higher kind of life, an added life; that very life of which the same writer says in Second Corinthians 4:11: "his life [is] revealed in our mortal body."

Now have we any precedents for this in the Scriptures? Certainly. We go back to the story of Samson, and we find that his strength was not produced by muscle and bone or weight and size, but by the Holy Spirit. When the Spirit began "to move upon him," he suddenly developed gigantic strength and slew his enemies and carried away the gates of their cities and laughed at their strength and numbers. And when by disobedience he lost the Holy Spirit and sank into self-indulgence and sin his body became as weak as a child's and his enemies blinded him and made sport of him.

I once found myself in an abandoned office where I had some work to do at night. There was neither light nor heat. I lit a match and tried to light the gas, but the pipes had been taken out. I then searched for lamps and candles but there were none. Finally I went to a closet where I had been accustomed to keep old newspapers, and I felt sure if I could throw these in the grate I would have at least temporary light. But the newspapers had already been thrown into the grate and there was nothing left but a heap of black and lifeless ashes. Then I discovered a small bottle of kerosene. I poured it in on the ashes in the grate and they blazed up, lighting the room and dispelling the chill, and I was able to finish my work with comfort. As often as the grate fire began to go down all I had to do was to pour a little fresh oil upon it. That is the parable of the Spirit's quickening life in our mortal bodies. Our natural bodies may be like that heap of dead ashes. But if the Spirit is dwelling in us we will live by His life until our work is done.

Seventeenth Day

THE SPIRIT
OF TRUTH

Another Counselor . . . the Spirit of Truth.
(John 14:16–17)

The Holy Spirit has given us His supreme
message in the Holy Scriptures. The Bible is
the standard of spiritual truth, and in all His
teachings and leadings, the Holy Ghost never
contradicts His own Word. They who are most
fully led of the Spirit will always most reverence
the authority of the Scriptures, and walk in the
most perfect conformity with their principles and
precepts.

But it is not enough to have the letter of the
Word; He who gave it must also interpret it and
make it spirit and life. It is His to unfold to the
heart the power and reality of the written Word

70

and to bring it to our remembrance in the opportune moment as the lamp of guidance, or the sword of defense in the hour of temptation.

A prominent member of the House of Representatives, speaking the other day about the inestimable value of the National Library of Congress, was asked how it was possible for a busy member, without much study and labor, to know how to use it effectually, and to be able always to find the right volume or page where a given subject was discussed. "Oh," he replied, "that is made perfectly easy for us by our invaluable librarian, who knows every book and subject, and all we have to do is to send a little page from our desk in the House with a note to him requesting the best authority on any subject we require, and he immediately comes back with the right book and the leaves turned down at the very spot where we need the information." Blessed be God, we have a Divine Librarian who understands the Bible better than we ever can, and who has come to be our Monitor and Guide, not only into its meaning, but also into its practical application to every need of life.

It is not enough to have a good light, we must have the organs of vision or it is of no use; and we must have them in perfect condition. Now, the Holy Spirit comes to be to us sight as well as light.

This is the special work of the Holy Ghost, to give to us a new spiritual vision and organ of apprehension, so that the soul directly perceives divine things and realities. Perhaps the first effect of this divine illumination is that the things of God become intensely real, and stand out with vividness and distinctness, like figures cut in relief on the wall. The person of Christ, the light of His countenance, the distinct sweetness of His Spirit, the "peace which transcends all understanding," "the joy of the Lord," the heavenly world, all become to the heart more actual and intensely vivid than the things we see with our outward eyes, and touch with our human hands.

In the first chapter of Ephesians, the Apostle Paul has given us a sublime view of the effect of this inward illumination upon the heart.

I have not stopped remembering you in my prayers. I keep asking that the God of our Lord Jesus Christ, the glorious Father, may give you the Spirit of wisdom and revelation, so that you may know him better. I pray also that the eyes of your heart may be enlightened in order that you may know the hope to which he has called you, the riches of his glorious inheritance in the saints, and his incomparably great power for us who believe. That power is like the working of his mighty strength, which he exerted in Christ when he raised him from the dead and seated him at his right hand in the heavenly realms, far above all rule and authority, power and dominion, and every title that can be given, not only in the present age but also in the

one to come. And God placed all things
under his feet . . .

. . . in order that in the coming ages he might
show the incomparable riches of his grace,
expressed in his kindness to us in Christ
Jesus. (1:16–22a, 2:7)

Here we find it is not the eyes of our intellect,
but the eyes of the heart that are to be illuminated, and when so quickened by the Spirit
of revelation in the knowledge of Him, we shall
understand what is the hope of our calling, and
the glorious privileges and prospects which we
are to inherit in Christ.

And we shall see that the riches of the glory of
His inheritance are not only for us, but in us, and
even in us now. We shall be stirred with a realization of the exceeding greatness of His power
toward us and for us. We shall have an adequate
conception of the mighty things that we may dare
to claim of Him, and we shall learn to:

Rise with our risen Lord,
Ascend with Christ above
And in the heavenlies dwell with Him
Whom seeing not we love.

THE SPIRIT OF WISDOM

He will guide you into
all truth. (John 16:13)

The Holy Spirit is promised to us as our personal Guide in the path of life. "Those who
are led by the Spirit of God are sons of God"
(Romans 8:14). Some persons are so zealous for
the Word of God that they deny any direct
guidance of the Spirit apart from the Word, but if
we truly believe the Word itself we will be forced
to accept its distinct statements, that the personal
presence of God is given to the humble and
obedient disciple for the needed direction in
every step of life. "I will instruct you and teach
you in the way you should go;/ I will counsel you
and watch over you" (Psalm 32:8). "The Lord will

74

guide you always" (Isaiah 58:11a). "When he has brought out all his own, he goes on ahead of them, and his sheep follow him because they know his voice" (John 10:4). "In all your ways acknowledge him,/ and he will make your paths straight" (Proverbs 3:6).

We find the Apostle Paul constantly recognizing the personal direction of the Holy Spirit even in matters where there was no distinct direction in the Word. The whole course of Paul's missionary journeys was ordered by the personal direction of the Lord. "Being sent forth," we are told, "by the Holy Ghost," he and Barnabas sailed unto Cyprus. A little later the same Spirit restrained them from preaching in Bithynia and Asia, and led them from Troas to Philippi, to begin their European ministry. Still later, we are told that he "purposed in the Spirit" to go to Jerusalem and Rome, and none of the perils of the way could afterward turn him aside from that which had come to him as the voice of God.

The Spirit guides us by the Scriptures, by their general principles and teachings, and by bringing to us special passages from the Word, either through the law of mental suggestion, and impressing them upon our heart, or by various ways fitted to emphasize a passage as a divine message to our hearts.

He also directs us by His own direct voice when necessary; and yet we must not expect the special and remarkable intimations of the Holy Ghost at all times, or when we have sufficient light from other sources. There is danger of fanaticism here. We have no right to ask God to give us a special revelation of His will where either the light of our own common sense or the teaching of Scripture has already made the matter sufficiently plain.

The Holy Spirit guides us most frequently by intuitions of our sanctified judgment, and the conclusion of our minds, to which He leads us with the quiet assurance of acting in perfect freedom and naturalness, and yet of being influenced by the presence and suggestion of His own Spirit. Under such circumstances the mind and judgment are perfectly simple and natural.

The truly consecrated spirit may expect to be thus held and influenced by the Divine wisdom; and it will often find itself restrained from things by an inward reluctance, or repulsion, which it cannot fully explain, and led to other things by a strong and distinct inclination and sense of rightness and fitness which afterwards prove, by the result, to have been the directing presence of God.

We are sometimes taught that we are guided by providence. A devout mind will, of course, always have regard to the external providence of God, and will be habitually watching to see His hand in everything that occurs; but it would be very dangerous to allow ourselves to be directed by outward events apart from the distinct leadings of God in our spirit and by His Word. Quite as frequently we will find ourselves led to go in the face of circumstances as to follow the favoring gales of outward events. Most of the important events and accomplished purposes in the lives of God's servants, as recorded in the Scriptures, were in direct opposition to all the circumstances that were occurring around them.

Let us notice also some of the principles and conditions of divine guidance.

The first is a surrendered spirit. Next, there must be a readiness to obey. He will not give us light unless we mean to follow it. Then we must trust His guidance. We must believe that He is with us and directing us. We must lean upon His arm with all our heart, and implicitly look up into His face and expect Him to be true to us. We must also have "trained [our] selves to distinguish good from evil" (Hebrews 5:14b).

Sometimes our mistakes will become most instructive to us by showing us the places where we have erred, and save us from repeating the mistake afterwards with more serious consequences. We must learn to distinguish between mere impressions and the deeper convictions of the entire judgment under the light of the Spirit, and between the voice of the Shepherd and that of the spirit of error.

This He will teach us, and teach us more and more perfectly through experience. We will have to learn also to walk with Him when we cannot understand the way.

> Through waves and clouds and storms
> He gently clears thy way;

Wait then His time, so shall thy night
Soon end in glorious day.

Nineteenth Day

THE SPIRIT OF COMFORT

Walking in the comfort of
the Holy Ghost. (Acts 9:31, KJV)

Our English translators have given to the Greek word "Paraclete," which the Lord Jesus applied to the Holy Ghost, the translation of the Comforter. And while this term is not expressive of the complete sense of the original, yet it expresses very beautifully one of the most blessed characters and offices of the Holy Spirit.

He is the Spirit of peace. It is twofold peace, peace with God, and the peace of God. We find many references to this twofold rest. "Come to me, all you who are weary and burdened, and I will give you rest" (Matthew 11:28). This is the rest which the troubled soul receives when it comes to Christ for pardon. But then there is a deeper rest: "Take my yoke upon you and learn from me, for I am gentle and humble in heart, and you will find rest for your souls" (29). This is experienced after the surrender of the will to God, and the discipline of the Spirit fully received.

There is a deeper peace, so we find the risen Savior meeting the disciples in the upper room with the salutation, "Peace be with you," as He shows them His hands and His side: but later, He breathes on them and adds a second benediction of peace as they receive the Holy Ghost. It is the special gift of the Holy Ghost; nay, it is rather His own personal abiding, as the Dove of Rest, spreading His tranquil wings over the troubled sea of human strife and passion, and bringing His own everlasting rest.

He is the Spirit of Joy. This is a deeper and fuller spring, but the source is the same, the bosom of the Comforter. "The kingdom of God," we are told, "is not a matter of eating and drinking, but righteousness, peace and joy in the Holy Spirit" (Romans 14:17). This is the joy of Christ Himself. It is the Spirit's business to take the things that are Christ's and reveal them to us. And so the Master has said, "I have told you this so that my joy may be in you and that your joy may be complete" (John 15:11). "Until now you have not asked for anything in my name. Ask and you will receive, and your joy will be complete" (John 16:24). We have some conception of His joy. This is the joy He will give to us. It is nothing less than the fullness of His own heart throbbing in our breast and sharing with us His own immutable blessedness.

This joy is wholly independent of surrounding circumstances or natural temperament. It is a spirit of native cheerfulness, but it is a perennial fountain of divine gladness, springing up from sources that lie far below the soil of human nature.

He is the spirit of comfort and consolation. It is especially in the hour of distress and trial that the Comforter becomes manifest in His peculiar ministry of consolation and love. It is then that the promise is fulfilled which applies more especially to this person of the Godhead as the very Mother of the soul.

The comfort is in proportion to the trial. There is a blessed equilibrium of joy and sorrow. "For just as the sufferings of Christ flow over into our lives, so also through Christ our comfort overflows" (2 Corinthians 1:5). As far as the pendulum swings backward, it swings forward. Every trial is, therefore, a prophecy of blessing to the heart that walks with Jesus. Times of trial are, therefore, often our times of greatest joy. God's nightingales sing at midnight, and:

> Sorrow touched by God grows bright
> With more than rapturous ray
> As darkness shows us worlds of light
> We never saw by day.

If we should know the full comfort of the Holy Spirit we must cooperate with Him, and rejoice by simple faith, often when our circumstances are all forbidding, and even our very feelings give no response of sympathy or conscious joy. It is a great thing to learn as James says, to "count it all joy" (1:2a, KJV). Counting is not the language of poetry or sentiment, but of cold, unerring calculation. It adds up the column thus: Sorrow, temptation, difficulty, opposition, depression, desertion, danger, discouragement on every side, but at the bottom of the column God's presence, God's will, God's joy, God's promise, God's recompense. "For our light and momentary troubles are achieving for us an eternal glory that far outweighs them all" (2 Corinthians 4:17). How much does the column amount to? The sum of all the addition is "ALL JOY," for "our present sufferings are not worth comparing with the glory that will be revealed in us" (Romans 8:18).

That is the way to count your joy. Singly, a given circumstance may not seem joyful, but counted in with God, and His presence and promise, it makes a glorious sum in the arithmetic of faith. We can rejoice in the Lord as an act of will, and when we do, the Comforter will soon bring all our emotions into line, and all our circumstances too.

WALKING IN THE SPIRIT

If we live in the Spirit let us walk in the Spirit. (Galatians 5:25, KJV)

What is it to walk in the Spirit? Generally, it may be said, it is to maintain the habit of dependence upon the Holy Ghost for our entire life: spirit, soul and body. We know what it is at times to enjoy His conscious presence. We live in the Spirit, we have felt the touch of His quickening life, now let us walk in the Spirit. Let us abide in this fellowship. Let us lean continually upon His strength, and drink unceasingly from His life, a babe from its mother's breast. But more particularly:

1. To walk in the Spirit is to recognize the Spirit as present and abiding in us. How often,

after we have asked His presence, we treat Him as if He had deceived us, and cry to Him as if He were afar off! Let us recognize Him as having come, and address Him as a present and indwelling friend. He will always meet our recognition.

2. It means to trust Him and count upon Him in the emergencies of life, to regard Him as one who has undertaken our cause and expects to be called upon in every time of need, and will unfailingly be found faithful and all-sufficient in every crisis. The very name Paraclete means one that we can always call upon and find at our side. We must trust the Holy Spirit and expect Him to respond to our need as implicitly as we expect the air to answer the opening of our lungs, and the sunrise to meet us in the morning. And yet how many treat the Holy Spirit as if He were a capricious and most unreliable friend! How many of our prayers are despairing groans or scolding reflections on His love and faithfulness!

3. We must consult the Holy Spirit if we would walk in the Spirit. We will often find that the things that seem most easy will fail and disappoint us when we rely upon their apparent probability and the mere promise of outward circumstances, and we will also find where we commit our way unto Him, and acknowledge Him in all our ways, that He will so direct our paths that the things which seemed most difficult and improbable, will become the easiest and the most successful. He would teach us thus to trust in Him with all our heart, and lean not on our own understanding; in

all our ways to acknowledge Him and He will direct our steps.

4. If we would walk in the Spirit we must obey Him when He does speak, and we must remember that the first part of obedience is to hearken. It is not enough to say we have done all we knew, we ought to know, and we may know, for He has said that we will know His voice, and if we do not it must be that we are to blame, or else God is responsible for our mistake. But this cannot be.

If we will be still and suppress our own impulses and clamorous desires, and will meet Him with a heart surrendered to His will and guidance, we will know His way. "He guides the humble in what is right/ and teaches them his way" (Psalm 25:9).

5. Walking in the Spirit implies that we will keep step with the Holy Ghost, and that our obedience will be so prompt that we shall never find ourselves a step behind Him, and following Him at a distance which we may find it hard to recover.

On our great railroads there are certain trains that run upon the highest possible schedule of time. The itinerary is so arranged that there is no margin allowed on which to overtake lost time, so that should the train be late, it is scarcely possible to overtake the interval lost. God has drawn the plan of our life on such a scale that there are no minutes left blank, and if we lose one, the next has no margin to afford for its recovery. All that we can crowd into the future will be needed for the future itself, and therefore if we lose a step there is danger that we will continue to be a step behind, and it will require the same exertion to keep up even a step behind as it would to walk abreast of God every moment.

He has given us a gentle, patient Guide, who is willing to go with us all the way, and come into the minutest steppings of our life. Let us take heed that we grieve Him not away nor miss any of His gentle will. Let us be sensitive to His touch, responsive to His whisper, obedient to His commandments, and able ever to say, "He has not left me alone, for I always do what pleases him" (John 8:29b).

Twenty-first Day

PRAYING IN THE SPIRIT

Pray in the Holy Spirit. (Jude 1:20)

The mystery of prayer! There is nothing like it in the natural universe. A higher and a lower being in perfect communion. A familiar intercourse, yet both as widely distinct as the finite is from the infinite. More wonderful even than that we should be able to hold converse with the insect that crawls beneath our feet, or the bird that flutters on the branches at our window! Marvelous bond of prayer that can span the gulf between the Creator and the creature, the infinite God and the humblest and most illiterate child!

How has this been accomplished? The three Divine persons have all cooperated in opening the gates of prayer. The Father waits at the throne of grace as the hearer of prayer. The Son has come to reveal the Father, and has returned to be our Advocate in His presence. And the Holy Spirit has come still nearer, as the other Advocate in the heart, to teach us the heavenly secret of prayer, and send up our petitions in the true spirit to the hands of our heavenly Intercessor.

1. The Holy Spirit reveals to us our needs. This is always the first element in prayer, a painful consciousness of failure and necessity. The Spirit of prayer is the spirit of dependence and conscious need.

2. The Holy Spirit next awakens in the soul holy desires for the blessings that God is about to give. Desire is an element in prayer. "Whatever you ask for in prayer," our Lord says, "believe that you have received it" (Mark 11:24). These deep, spiritual longings are like the rootlets by which the plant draws the nourishments from the soil; like the absorbing vessels of the human system, which take in and assimilate nourishment and food. The desires give intensity and force to our prayer, and enlarge the heart to receive the blessing when it comes. God, therefore, often keeps His children waiting for the visible answer to their petitions, in order that they may the more ardently desire the blessing, and be thus enabled to receive it more fully and appreciate it more gratefully when it comes.

3. The Holy Spirit lays upon the heart wherein He dwells the special burden of prayer. We often read in the old prophetic Scripture of "the burden

of the Lord." And so still the Lord lays His burden on His consecrated messengers. This is the
meaning of the strong language of the text, "The
Spirit himself intercedes for us with groans that
words cannot express" (Romans 8:26b). Sometimes this burden is inarticulate and unintelligible
even to the supplicant himself.

It is not necessary that we should always know.
Indeed, perhaps we will never fully know what
any of our prayers wholly mean. God's answer is
always larger than our petition, and even when
our prayer is most definite and intelligent there is
a wide margin which only the Holy Ghost can interpret, and God will fill it up in His infinite wisdom and love. That is what is meant by the
significant language of the text, "And he who
searches our hearts knows the mind of the Spirit,
because the Spirit intercedes for the saints in accordance with God's will" (27). The Father is always searching our hearts and listening, not to
our wild and often mistaken outcries, but to the
mind of the Holy Spirit in us, whom He recognizes as our true guardian and monitor, and He
grants us according to His petitions and not
merely our words.

The sensitive spirit grows very quick to discern
God's voice. That which would naturally be con-
sidered as simple depression of spirit comes to be
instantly recognized as a hint that God has something to say to us, or something to ask in us for
ourselves or others. If we were but more watchful
we would find that nothing comes to us at any

moment of our lives which has not some divine significance, and which does not lead us in some way to communion or service.

4. The Spirit brings to our hearts, in the ministry of prayer, the encouragement of God's Word, the promise of His grace, and the fullness of Christ to meet our need. It is He who gives us such conceptions of Christ as awaken in us confidence of blessing. He opens to our vision the infinite resources of the grace of God, and shows us all the rich provision of our Father's house.

Thus He is in us the Spirit of faith, the Spirit of adoption, the Spirit of liberty in prayer, the Spirit of holy confidence and enlargement of heart, and the witnessing Spirit, who, when we pray in faith, seals upon our soul the divine assurance that our prayer is accepted before God, and that the answer will be surely given. Our Lord always requires this faith as the condition of answered prayer. "Whatever you ask for in prayer, believe that you have received it, and it will be yours" (Mark 11:24). "When he asks, he must believe and not doubt, because he who doubts is like a wave of the sea, blown and tossed by the wind. That man should not think he will receive anything from the Lord" (James 1:6–7).

5. The Holy Spirit will also teach us when to cease from prayer, and turn our petition into thanksgiving, or go out in obedience to meet the answer as it waits before us, or comes to meet us.

A POT OF OIL

Elisha replied to her, "How can I help you?
Tell me, what do you have in your house?"
"Your servant has nothing there at all,"
she said, "except a little oil." (2 Kings 4:2)

The passage before us is a striking object lesson of the Holy Ghost in His all-sufficiency for the supplying of every source of need.

First, we have, in the case of this poor widow, an example of great need. Her situation was one of debt, danger, distress and of complete helplessness.

Nearly all the great examples of faith and victorious grace which we find in the Scriptures came out of situations of extremity and distress. God loves hard places, and faith is usually born of danger and extremity.

Was there, then, nothing left for her? Was she entirely without resources? "Tell me, what do you have in your house?" And she answered, "Your servant has nothing there at all, except a little oil." To her that seemed nothing, and yet it contained the supply of all her need.

But that little pot of oil was not a little thing. It represented the power of the Holy Ghost, the infinite attribute of God Himself.

We need not stop to prove that oil is the scriptural symbol of the Holy Spirit. And so this little vessel of oil represented the presence and power of the Spirit, which every believer may have, and in some measure does have, and which, if we only know how to use Him, is equal to every possible situation and need of our Christian life. But in how many cases is this an unrealized power and an unemployed force?

There is a grim story told of a poor Scotchwoman who went to her pastor in her extremity, and told him of her poverty. He kindly asked her if she had no friend or member of her family who could support or help her, and she said she had a son, a bonny lad, but he was in India, in the service of the government. "But does he write to you?" "Oh, yes; he often writes me, and sends the kindest letters, and such pretty pictures in them. But I am too proud to tell him how poor I am, and, of course, I have not expected him to send me money." "Would you mind showing me some of the pictures?" said the minister. And so Janet went to her Bible, and brought out from between the leaves a great number of Bank of England notes, laid away with the greatest care. "These," she said, "are the pictures." The minister smiled, and said, "Janet, you are richer than I am. These are bank notes; and every one of them might have been turned into money, and you have had all your needs supplied. You have had a fortune in your Bible without knowing it." Alas, beloved, many of us have fortunes in our Bibles without knowing it, or using our infinite resources!

The Holy Spirit is given to us to be used for every sort of need, and yet, with all the power of heaven at our call, many of us are going about in starvation, simply because we do not know our treasure, and do not use our redemption rights.

But she must make room. She must get vessels, and empty vessels, to hold the supply which is about to be revealed. And so our greatest need is to make room for God.

Again, there must be faith to count upon God and go forward expecting Him to meet our need. And so she did not wait till the oil was running over from her little pot. But she provided the vessels in advance and acted as though she had an unbounded supply.

She showed her faith by beginning to pour out the contents of the little pot into the larger vessel. And as she poured, it continued to flow and overflow until every vessel was filled, and still that little pot was running, and it might have been running still if there had been room enough to hold its multiplying stream.

So faith must go forward and act out its confidence and risk itself by doing something and putting itself in the place where God must meet it with actual help. It was when the water at Cana was poured out that it became wine. It was when the man stretched out his hand that it was healed. It was as the lepers went on their way that they were made whole. It was as the father went back to his home that the messenger was sent to tell him that his son was alive.

There is yet another lesson, the most important of all: "Go, sell the oil and pay your debts. You and your sons can live on what is left." The oil was but the representative of value, and was convertible into everything that she could need. And so the Holy Ghost is convertible into everything that we can require.

There is a parallel passage in the Gospels of Matthew and Luke which teaches a great lesson. In the one passage it reads, "If you, then, though you are evil, know how to give good gifts to your children, how much more will your Father in Heaven give the Holy Spirit to those who ask Him." In the parallel passage in the other Gospel, instead of the Holy Spirit, it reads, "Give good gifts to those who ask Him." That is to say, the Holy Ghost gives all good gifts and He is equivalent to anything and everything that we need.

The oil did not stop until the woman stopped; God was still working when her faith reached its limit. And the same God is working still.

NEW IDEALS THROUGH THE COMFORTER

Till the Spirit is poured upon us from on high,/ and the desert becomes a fertile field,/ and the fertile field seems like a forest. (Isaiah 32:15)

When the Comforter comes in His fullness, He not only changes the desert into a fertile field, but even "the fertile field seems like a forest." This is a very remarkable expression and the obvious meaning is that so great will be the transformation of the church, and of the Christian life of the individual, that the vision we have hitherto known will seem as nothing in comparison with the blessing that is to come. Even

95

the fruitful valley will be so improved that it will seem as if it had only been a forest before.

One of the worst features of the private and public life even of the people of God is the tendency to sink into ruts and to grow rigid and frigid in the formal, conventional routine of life. The old proverb, "Good enough is never good," is in place here. No doubt the reason so little progress is made by very many persons is because they are measuring themselves by old standards and really never getting any further on. When the Holy Spirit comes, He lifts our minds to new ideals and gives us conceptions of things so much in advance of our present experiences that we long for higher ground; the saved become sanctified and the sanctified rise to a life of sacrifice and unselfish service.

Sometimes God permits us to see in some other life the glorious possibilities that we are missing and we rise up to new planes, new ambitions, new visions and new commissions of service for God and man. Again he declares in the second chapter of First Corinthians,

> "No eye has seen,
>   no ear has heard,
> no mind has conceived
>   what God has prepared for those who love
>   him,"
> but God has revealed it to us by his Spirit.
> (9–10)

When this vision comes there rises before us the alluring prospect of that better country which Christ is waiting to bring us into:

> We stand, and from the mountain top
> See all the land below.
> Rivers of milk and honey rise
> And all the fruit of paradise,
> In endless plenty grow.

There is a thrilling story told of a man of great wealth and brilliant genius who had become a leader in the industrial life of the land, and the master of an enormous fortune, but who had no taste for art or music or high things. One day he was called upon by an old schoolmate from the distant land where both were born and who in turn had become illustrious in his profession as a musician. He invited the merchant prince to come to one of his concerts and hear him play on his famous violin, but the millionaire laughed at him and said he had no time for such trifles; he was engaged in more practical things. At last the musician caught his friend by strategy. He took his violin one day to the factory of the rich man, and asked him to make some trifling repairs upon it, as he was a machinist while the other was only a musician. After the trifling work had been done, the musician began to play to see if it was all right, but before half a dozen bars of music had been rolled off, the millionaire was standing with the tears streaming down his face with undisguised admiration and delight. The music had broken his heart and the musician had conquered him by his wiles. Not only so, the whole factory became demoralized, and as he played on, the entrancing strains gathered clerks, foreman, porters, everybody, in crowds around the door, and at last the musician apologized for disturbing their business; but the great man, wiping the tears from his eyes, said, "Don't stop for the world. Play on; I never knew till this moment how much I had missed out of my life." Poor man, he found that day a new world of sweetness to which he had been a stranger, and his heart longed for more.

In a far higher sense that is what happens when the light of heaven falls upon the heart and we "see the king in his beauty/ and view a land that stretches afar" (Isaiah 33:17). Then earthly things pale before the vision of that better country and our hearts long for God and heaven. Oh, if we should go on in our blindness until it is too late! Oh, if some day we should wake to hear "the sound . . . like that of harpists playing their harps" (Revelation 14:26), and the new song they sing above, and discover at last that we have no part in it, but have thrown our lives away upon the barren, empty wilderness of life, ours would be the eternal sorrow and an irretrievable loss!

Let us ask God to open our vision, to waken our hearts, to show us the things that are true and good and beautiful and everlasting, the things which "no eye has seen,/ no ear has heard,/ no mind has conceived" but which "God has prepared for those who love him," and which "God has revealed to us by his Spirit" (1 Corinthians 2:9–10).

Oh, that the great Revealer might come to us and show us the vision! Oh, that the great Inspirer might come to us and lift our hearts to meet it!

Twenty-fourth Day

THE GIFTS
OF THE SPIRIT
AND THE GRACE
OF LOVE

*But eagerly desire the greater gifts. And
now I will show you the most excellent way.
If I speak in the tongues of men and of
angels, but have not love, I am only a
resounding gong or a clanging cymbal.*
(1 Corinthians 12:31–13:1)

Much attention is being given at this time to
the supernatural gifts of the Spirit. No
Bible Christian can for a moment question the
value and permanency of these gifts which the
apostle describes so fully in the 12th chapter of
First Corinthians. There is every reason to

believe that all these gifts were meant to be in operation in the Church of Christ until the end of the age and there is an apparent revival of several of them at the present time. But along with this we sometimes hear the teaching of the extreme view that these supernatural gifts, and especially the one most in evidence of late, the gift of tongues, are essential evidences of the baptism of the Holy Spirit. This is most unscriptural.

In the first place the teaching referred to is sure to lead people to seek for manifestations and peculiar experiences rather than for God Himself, and thus decentralize and distract the heart from its supreme goal. In the next place such teaching is directly contrary to the emphatic statements of the apostle that the Holy Spirit exercises His sovereignty in bestowing these gifts on whomever He will. He knows the particular forms of divine enduement that are best suited for our different ministries and qualifications. More important still such a view would place undue emphasis on the gifts of power rather than the spirit of love and turn us aside from the practical and useful to the sensational.

The true scriptural attitude is to make the Lord Jesus Himself the central object of our thought and affection, to seek to be filled with His Spirit, for His service and glory, to cultivate the disposition of love and the graces that tend to make us a blessing to others and to trust Him to give to us and to others whatever special gifts He sees to be best suited in His great plan for each of our lives.

The exercise of these supernatural gifts in Christian work and worship is carefully regulated by the apostle in the 14th chapter of First Corinthians. Certain principles are clearly laid down that should control the worship of the assembly. The first of these is edification. Nothing should be encouraged that does not tend to promote the spiritual good of the largest number. The second is order. All confusion, extravagance and exaggerated emotion should be avoided. The third is self-control. "The spirits of prophets are subject to the control of prophets" (1 Corinthians 14:32). Even the Holy Spirit does not take away our mental poise or expect us to surrender our common sense and will or yield ourselves to any hypnotic influence. But above all else we are exhorted to seek for the grace of love. Not only is it the highest end to be pursued but it is the surest means of accomplishing the very end that many are pursuing, a deeper filling of the Spirit. The apostle says, "I will show you the most excellent way" (1 Corinthians 12:31), that is a better way for obtaining the blessing you seek. That way is to forget yourself in a spirit of love and the purpose of being a blessing to others. The poet Lowell has given a fine illustration of this thought.

In the beautiful poem of Sir Launfal, a Christian knight had gone forth with holy zeal in quest of that which represented in that age the most glorious gift of God. It was the Holy Grail, the identical cup from which the Lord Jesus and His disciples had drunk the sacred draught "on the night He was betrayed" (1 Corinthians 11:23). As he passed out from the palace gate, a loathsome leper stretched out his festering hands for help, and begged him to take the filthy cup that was lying beside him, and bring him a drink of water from the flowing brook. But the knight waved him aside and swept on, for he was after higher things.

Years passed by, as he pursued in vain his weary quest over many lands and under scorching suns. His body was worn, his hair was gray, his heart was broken, his hopes had almost died. A worn-out wreck, he was slowly returning to his home with a crushed and disappointed heart, when once again a leper met him on the way and stretched out the same festering hands for the same loving ministry. Swiftly the knight leaped from his horse, picked up the repulsive vessel, and hastening to the stream, with profoundest courtesy and tenderest sympathy he handed to the sufferer the drink he had requested. In a moment the scene was changed, and the transfigured leper had become none other than the Son of Man Himself. The light of heaven shone around Him and the filthy cup became transformed into a shining vessel of silver; and as the Master handed it back to him it was indeed the "Holy Grail!" Yes, he had found the more excellent way. So may we seek and find.

Twenty-fifth Day

THE SPIRIT OF REVIVAL

For I will pour water on the thirsty land,
and streams [floods] on the dry ground.
(Isaiah 44:3)

Two forms of the Spirit's operations are here set forth, the ordinary and the extraordinary. Even the ordinary work of the Spirit is expressed by the strongest figure, "I will pour water," but His extraordinary ministry is described by a more emphatic figure, "I will pour streams [floods] on the dry ground." These floods represent the occasional outpouring of the Spirit of God in seasons of great revival which the Church is witnessing now in many places and which earnest Christian hearts are longing to see everywhere.

Such seasons of mighty blessing are powerful

witnesses for God, awakening the attention of a careless world and compelling even the most sceptical and indifferent to recognize the reality and power of the gospel of Jesus Christ. Such seasons, for a time at least, lift up a standard against the enemy and check the prevalence and power of evil as no mere human words or authorities ever can. God becomes His own witness and the scoffer and the sinner are awed and humbled before the majesty of the Lord. Let us pray for such a mighty outpouring of the Holy Ghost in our day. We are warranted to expect such manifestations of divine power especially as the coming of our Lord draweth nigh. These are to be the very signs that will herald His return, "I will pour out my Spirit on all people" (Acts 2:17a), He says, "I will show wonders . . . before the coming of the great and dreadful day of the Lord" (19–20).

The prophet describes the individual blessing that will follow these gracious outpourings.

1. Conversions. "One will say, 'I belong to the Lord'" (Isaiah 44:5a). The Holy Spirit will lead souls, one by one, to Christ. How beautiful it is to read in the account of the Welsh revival of people springing up all over the meeting spontaneously and confessing the Savior they had just found. It was not through preaching, but through personal dealing with the Holy Spirit who was present pleading with souls all over the place, and they yielded and confessed Him one by one just as they settled the great transaction. Anyone can be

saved the moment he is ready to confess Christ as his Savior: "If you confess with your mouth, 'Jesus is Lord,' and believe in your heart that God raised him from the dead, you will be saved" (Romans 10:9). This is a personal confession directly to God and He accepts it and records the name of the confessor in the Lamb's book of life.

2. Confession. "Another will call himself by the name of Jacob" (Isaiah 44:5a). This undoubtedly represents the identifying of the individual with the Lord's people. When the Holy Spirit truly leads souls to Christ, they always want to belong to His people. How quickly all censorious criticism about churches and church members disappears and the true and humble spirit turns to the children of God for fellowship, sympathy and help. It is the duty of the young convert to attach himself to the fold of Christ, and although there may be many imperfections in the visible church, yet it is far safer to be inside than outside and all who truly love the Master will want to be identified with some branch of His cause.

3. Consecration. "Still another will write on his hand, 'the Lord's' " (Isaiah 44:5a). This represents that closer covenant into which it is the privilege of the individual soul to enter with the Lord Jesus. Dr. Phillip Dodridge recommends to young Christians to write down their covenant and formally sign it and ratify it, and then preserve it, and he suggests a very solemn form in which the soul may give itself to the Lord and claim His covenant blessing.

There is no doubt that such personal covenants have brought great blessings to those that have faithfully kept them and as we look back upon the records of our own lives we shall find that even where we have failed "He will remain faithful" (2 Timothy 2:13b).

4. Higher spiritual blessing. The next clause, "and will take the name Israel" (Isaiah 44:5b), seems to express the highest spiritual experiences. Israel stands for much more than Jacob. It marks the second of the patriarch's spiritual life when the Supplanter became the Prince of God. When the Holy Spirit comes, He leads the willing heart in the deeper and highest things of God. He shows the young convert that it is his privilege to be baptized with the Holy Ghost, to receive the Lord Jesus as an indwelling presence, to be delievered from the power of self and sin and to enter into a life of abiding victory, rest and power.

Indeed, these are among the richest fruits of every true revival, and no wise Christian worker will be satisfied until the souls committed to his care have been led into all the fullness of Christ. This is presented here as a voluntary act and as the privilege of all who are willing to rise to it. God does not force His best things upon us, but offers them to our holy ambition.

Will we, as we realize this mighty promise, rise to it for ourselves and claim, even as we read these lines, these showers of blessing, these floods of power and these glorious fruits for our own individual Christian life and the cause and kingdom of our Lord.

Twenty-sixth Day

THE SPIRIT OF
THE ADVENT

The Spirit and the bride say "Come!"
(Revelation 22:17a)

The great business of the Holy Ghost since Christ's ascension has been to prepare for His return. The two last messages of our departing Master, recorded in the first 10 verses of the Acts of the Apostles, are the promise of the Holy Ghost and the promise of His second coming. Between these two promises lies the whole Christian age, and the object of the first is to fulfill the last.

The Holy Ghost has now unfolded the prophetic vision, and as He closes it until the end of time, He pours out one ardent prayer and unites the beloved Bride of Jesus in it, "Come,

Lord Jesus." And then He sends the message forth to all around, and adds, "let him who hears say 'come' " (17a). And, turning to the world and the sinner, He utters the last message of inviting mercy to come to Jesus. "Whoever is thirsty, let him come; and whoever wishes, let him take the free gift of the water of life" (17b).

This passage suggests the connection of the Holy Ghost with the Lord's return.

1. The Holy Ghost has given us the predictions of Christ's second coming. Much of it we have misunderstood, much of it may remain somewhat obscure until the time of the end, but nothing has been left unsaid that we need to know to fit us for the meeting with our Lord.

2. The Holy Ghost has interpreted and illuminated the prophetic Scriptures.

Daniel uttered these advent visions, but he dimly comprehended them, and was told to seal them up until the time of the end. But he was also told that as the end drew near, the wise should understand, and this is just what is happening today.

The most remarkable sign that we are in the last days, and that the mystery of the ages is about to be finished, is the wondrous light which the Holy Ghost has shed on the interpretation of prophecy in our time.

3. The Holy Ghost is preparing for the Lord's coming by awakening the desire and expectation of Christ's return in the hearts of His disciples.

As the hour draws near this will become more

uniform and universal among the little flock, and when He appears His Bride will not be left "in darkness so that this day should surprise [her] like a thief" (1 Thessalonians 5:4), but she will be found ready and waiting to go forth to meet him.

Let us listen to His whisper, let us catch his full meaning, let us, as the day draws near, be found "bending ourselves back," and "lifting up our heads" and, like the bird upon the branch, with fluttering wings and uplifted eye waiting for the signal of its mate, let us be ready at His earliest call to rise to meet Him in the air.

4. The Holy Ghost is preparing for Christ's return by the spiritual enrobing of His children.

The call is going forth. " 'For the wedding of the Lamb has come,/ and his bride has made herself ready./ Fine linen, bright and clean, was given her to wear.'/ (Fine linen stands for the righteous acts of the saints)" (Revelation 19:7b–8).

The Holy Ghost is preparing a people today for the coming of Christ. There is a marked movement in all sections of the Christian Church toward separation from the world and entire consecration to Christ, that we may receive the baptism of the Holy Ghost and be transformed and conformed to Christ.

This is the very sign that the Bridegroom is near at hand. When the Bride is found robed and ready, her Lord will not be long behind.

Have you received the wedding robe? Have you made sure of the oil in your vessel with your lamp? Are you arrayed in raiment not only "clean" but also "bright," not only without the stain of sin, but with all the beauty and glory of the priestly garments?

5. The Holy Ghost is working in the providence of God among the nations, to prepare for the coming of Christ.

The wonderful events of our time are the beginning of those overturnings which are to bring in the kingdom of Christ and His millennial reign. The Ancient of Days is already working among the nations, and through the power of the Spirit of God is breaking down the barriers and opening up the highway for Christ's return.

6. The Holy Ghost is sending forth the disciples of Christ to fulfill their great trust in witnessing for Christ and evangelizing the world.

This is His greatest work of preparation for the coming of Christ. In direct connection with the promise of the Spirit is the great commission, "You will receive power when the Holy Spirit comes on you; and you will be my witnesses . . . to the ends of the earth" (Acts 1:8).

And so today we witness the mighty workings of the Holy Ghost, in sending out the message of the gospel to the neglected at home and the unreached abroad.

Beloved, if we are truly filled with the Holy Ghost and longing for the coming of Christ, we shall be active witnesses and workers in preparing for Him. We will be soul winners at home, and if we cannot go abroad we will help others go and give the gospel quickly to all the world.

THE SPIRIT
OF MISSIONS

*But you will receive power when the Holy
Spirit comes on you; and you will be my
witnesses . . . to the ends of the earth.*
(Acts 1:8)

This last promise of the Comforter from the
lips of our departing Lord connects the mission of the Spirit inseparably with the evangelization of the world. The book of Acts, which is
practically a following out of the thought
foreshadowed in this great promise, gives us
many fine illustrations of the Holy Spirit's
profound interests in sending the gospel to the
world.

In the first place the day of Pentecost itself was
a great missionary rally. The people that came

there and went from there were the representatives of every tribe and tongue, and they carried forth a missionary Pentecost and evangel to
all the world.

In the next place no sooner had the Holy Ghost
got the apostles sufficiently enlarged to go down
to Samaria and preach the gospel to their hated
cousins the result of which was an extraordinary
revival in Samaria, than the Spirit immediately
separated Philip, the leader of this revival, from
all His great and absorbing work there, and sent
him down to the desert for the one purpose of
carrying the gospel to a single Gentile hearer, the
prince of Ethiopia, and then sending back this
man to darkest Africa to be perhaps the pioneer
of Christianity in the heart of Ethiopia.

In the next place we find the blessed Spirit
taking infinite pains to get Peter out of His conventional narrowness and sufficiently expanded to
go as a missionary the next day to the Gentile
Cornelius where the second Pentecost came
down in mighty power and became the entering
wedge not only in Peter's mind but in the Apos-
tolic Council at Jerusalem for the opening of the
door of faith unto the Gentiles.

A little later we find the Holy Spirit organizing
a new church on cosmopolitan lines at Antioch as
a new center for the evangelization of the world.
From this large-hearted church the first great
missionary movement was sent forth a little later
and the two chief ministers of this church were
taken from all other work and dedicated to the

one business of preaching the gospel in the regions beyond.

But still the mighty thought of the Holy Spirit moves on and out on yet larger circles. The Council at Jerusalem, the first great ecclesiastical assembly of the Christian Church, is convened as a missionary convention for the purpose of settling the principles that are to regulate the new movement among the Gentile converts. The final deliverance of that great Council settles forever the foundations of Christian missions and states with inspired force and clearness the scope of the great missionary campaign of the Christian Church, namely, a visitation of the Gentiles in this present age for the purpose of gathering out of them a people for His name preparatory to the personal return of the Lord Jesus and the restoration of God's chosen people, Israel. Henceforth the church understands her business in this great missionary crusade. It is not to convert the world or bring about a millennium without Christ, but it is to select from every land a people for His name who will be prepared to welcome Him when He comes again.

Still the divine program moves on apace. Armed with this new missionary constitution the apostles go forth with fresh zeal and lay out a vast campaign, covering the whole of their own continent of western Asia and revisiting their former mission stations. Suddenly the Holy Spirit calls a halt. Their work was not pleasing to Him. Doubtless there were conversions, large congregations and faithful labors. But something was wrong. "They tried to enter Bithynia, but the Spirit of Jesus would not allow them to" (Acts 16:7). They were "kept by the Holy Spirit from preaching the word in the province of Asia" (6b). Wisely they heeded the divine check and tarried at Troas for further instructions. They soon came. In a night vision Paul beheld a man of Macedonia beckoning and calling, "Come over to Macedonia and help us" (9b). In the morning he related the vision and they communed and prayed about it and finally "gathered" that this must be the explanation of the check that had come upon their plans and that the Lord had a new commission and another field for them. It was a crisis more momentous than perhaps they realized. It simply meant that the old continent of Asia had had the gospel long enough for the present and that Europe now must have a chance. Europe was to be the continent of the future. Here were to arise the mighty political powers of the 20th century. The political center of gravity had changed and moved westward and the Church must follow.

So today the Holy Ghost, if we would but hear His voice, would call a halt on much of our religious activity and even our revival plans and the beckoning finger of the "Man of Macedonia" would call us to the new West which has arisen upon our horizon, the Pacific shore, the Sunrise Kingdom, China's millions and India's multitudes and would say to us "Arise from your religious selfishness, and if you would have the Pentecostal baptism in all its fullness go forth where the Comforter has already gone before you, and be my witnesses to the ends of the earth."

Twenty-eighth Day

FALSE AND
TRUE FIRE

Aaron's sons Nadab and Abihu took their
censers, put fire in them, and added in-
cense; and they offered unauthorized
[strange] fire before the Lord.
(Leviticus 10:1)

What a difference there is between fire and fire! What a difference between the fire that warms the hearth and cheers the home and the devouring flame that consumes the dwelling and leaves the homeless household shivering in the darkness and the cold!

What difference between the lightning stroke that shatters the tree, or strikes down some fugitive from the tempest that has taken refuge beneath its branches, and the same lightning when it has been caught in the electric battery or conveyed along the conducting wires as the motive power that runs our factories, carries our trolleys or conveys our messages.

Just as great is the difference between the true fire of the Holy Ghost and the flames of wild fanaticism and strange fire which the devil is kindling as his counterfeit wherever God is working.

1. The true fire is kindled at the Altar of Sacrifice. The false fire ignores the blood. There is much religious fire today which is merely the so-called "enthusiasm of humanity," or the emotion stirred by eloquence, art or zeal for some human cause and some selfish interest. It is not enough to believe in the Spirit, for spiritism and spiritualism all do this; but the true Spirit always comes in association with the blood.

2. The true fire is always found in the golden censer which represents the priesthood of the Lord Jesus Christ. While the altar represents His earthly sacrifice, the censer represents His heavenly intercession. Only through His name and meditation can sinful man find access to the presence of a holy God.

3. The true fire is kindled by the Holy Ghost and comes down from above. The false is earth born and comes from mere human emotion, intellectual culture, heart stirring eloquence or selfish zeal. It may even come from a spirit of fear and a guilty conscience.

4. The true fire is fed by the fuel of God's Word. The strange fire depends upon human

reasoning or interior revelations which come only from the *ignus fatuus* light of our own imagination.

The world is full of this kind of light and flame. We have the revelations of Spiritualism, the dreams of Theosophy and the *fatuus* fooleries of Christian Science. The desire of many people for a religion of feeling and a life guided by impulse rather than conviction and truth is the beginning of the same process and sure to lead eventually to the most dangerous delusions. There is no surer test of any religious experience than the simple Word of God.

5. The true fire not only descends from heaven, but goes back to heaven in a supreme purpose to glorify God, whereas the strange fire always seeks to exalt and promote the glory of some man or woman.

The more truly we are filled with the Holy Spirit, the more will we forget ourselves and seek the glory of Him that sent us. Whenever you see a religious movement or a religious leader trying to promote his fame, to demand his rights or to pose upon the stage of sensationalism and spectacular popularity, you may well say, "strange fire."

6. True fire purifies, while strange fire manifests itself in unhallowed forms of sinful indulgence and excess. The fire of the Holy Ghost instinctively seeks out every sinful thing and all that is of the flesh and the world and consumes it by a divine necessity.

7. The true fire warms and blesses, melts the heart into tenderness and inspires the soul with love. The false fire leads to criticism, division, censoriousness, harshness and judgment. James and John are the types of the latter seeking to call fire down from heaven to consume the people who refuse to honor and agree with him.

The fire of God is gentle, tender, loving, patient, free from self-assertion, strife and harshness, ready to make concessions, easy to get along with, and as sweet as it is strong.

8. The true fire works along the ordinary channels of duty while the false fire is apt to be eccentric, abnormal and extravagant. The true fire does not take people out of their place, but fits them better to fill it. It makes the mother a better mother, the pupil a better scholar, the employee a more faithful servant, the artisan a more skillful workman, the businessman more efficient in his calling, the worshiper more regular in his pew and systematic in his contributions and the Christian, whatever his place in the secular and spiritual world, more simple, practical and efficient in every sphere of duty and place of service. When people are struck with the false fire they become eccentric.

9. The true fire energizes and makes things go. The false fire is satisfied to watch its own blaze and hear its own report.

The Holy Ghost always puts the go in us and turns our blessing into the multiplied blessing of our fellowmen.

FILLED WITH THE SPIRIT

Be filled with the Spirit. (Ephesians 5:18)
And you have been given fullness in Christ.
(Colossians 2:10)

The emphatic word in both these verses is "filled." It is the Greek *pleroo*, which means to fill full, so full that there will be no room left empty. It does not mean to have a measure of the Holy Spirit, but to be wholly filled with, and possessed by, the Holy Ghost, and utterly lost in the life and fullness which constitutes the essence of the perfect blessing. A fountain half full will never become a spring. A river half full will never become a water power.

1. It is all connected with a living Person. We are not filled with an influence; we are not filled

with a sensation; we are not filled with a set of ideas and truth; we are not filled with a blessing, but we are filled with a Person. Christianity all centers in a living Person, and its very essence is the indwelling life of Christ Himself.

2. This Person is the true fullness of every part of our life.

He fills all the requirements of our salvation, all the conditions involved in connection with our redemption, reconciliation, justification.

And so we are "given fullness in Christ" (Colossians 2:10b). "Because by one sacrifice he has made perfect forever those who are being made holy" (Hebrews 10:14), and we are as fully saved as if we had never sinned.

Christ fills the deeper need of sanctification. He has provided for this in His atonement and in the resources of His grace. It is all wrapped up in Him, and must be received as a free and perfect gift through Him alone. "It is because of him that you are in Christ Jesus, who has become for us . . . holiness [sanctification, KJV] . . ." (1 Corinthians 1:30).

He is the fullness of our heart life. Christ will give us His heart as well as His Spirit, and will love in us with the love which loves the Lord God with all our heart, soul, strength and mind, and which loves one another as He loves us.

Christ will fill all the needs of our intellectual life. Our mental capacities will never know their full wealth of power and spiritual effectiveness until they become simply the vessels of His quickening life, and these brains of ours are laid at His feet simply as the censers which are to hold His holy fire. He will fill the needs of our body, for His body has been constituted, by the resurrection from the dead, a perpetual source of physical energy, sufficient for every physical function and every test of human life.

Christ will fill all the situations of providence and all the needs that arise in our secular callings and the circumstances of our daily life.

Finally, to be filled with Christ is not only to be filled with the Divine life in every part, but it is to be filled every moment. It is to take Him into the successive instants of our conscious existence and to abide in His fullness.

It is the secret of holiness. There is a measure of the Holy Spirit's life in every regenerate soul, but it is when every part of our being is filled with His love and possessed for His glory that we are wholly sanctified.

It is the secret of happiness. A heart half full is only full enough to make it conscious of its lack. It is when the cattle are filled that they lie down in the green pastures. "I have told you this so that my joy may be in you and that your joy may be complete [full]" (John 15:11).

It is the secret of power. The electric current can so fill a little wire that it will become a force to turn the great wheels of the factory, and the overflowing sluice of the village stream has power enough to run a score of factories all along the river banks, but it is simply because it is overflowing. Only full hearts accomplish effectual work for God. Only the overflow of our blessing blesses others.

For this reason I kneel before the Father, from whom his whole family in heaven and on earth derives its name. I pray that out of his glorious riches he may strengthen you with power through his Spirit in your inner being, so that Christ may dwell in your hearts through faith. And I pray that you, being rooted and established in love, may have power, together with all the saints, to grasp how wide and long and high and deep is the love of Christ, and to know this love that surpasses knowledge—that you may be filled to the measure of all the fullness of God.

Now to him who is able to do immeasurably more than all we ask or imagine, according to his power that is at work within us, to him be glory in the church and in Christ Jesus throughout all generations, for ever and ever! Amen. (Ephesians 3:14–21)

HOW TO RECEIVE THE COMFORTER

Receive the Holy Spirit. (John 20:22b)

The first condition of receiving the Spirit is a deep and intense desire.

An eastern caravan was overtaken once in the failure of the supply of water. The accustomed fountains were all dried, the oasis was a desert, and they halted an hour before sunset to find, after a day of scorching heat, that they were perishing for want of water. Vainly they explored the usual wells, for they were all dry. Dismay was upon all faces and despair in all hearts, when one of the ancient men approached the sheik and counseled him to unloose two beautiful harts that he was conveying home as a present to his bride, and let them scour the desert in search of water.

Their tongues were protruding with thirst, and their chests heaving with distress. But as they were led out to the borders of the camp and then set free on the boundless plain, they lifted up their heads on high, and sniffed the air with distended nostrils, and then, with unerring instinct, with course as straight as an arrow and speed as swift as the wind, they darted off across the desert. Swift horsemen followed close behind, and an hour or two later hastened back with the glad tidings that water had been found, and the camp moved with shouts of rejoicing to the happily discovered fountains.

So, still there is a heart that can ever find the springs of living water. It is the heart that hungers and thirsts for God.

2. The empty are always filled. "He has filled the hungry with good things, but has sent the rich away empty" (Luke 1:53), "Blessed are the poor in spirit, for theirs is the kingdom of heaven" (Matthew 5:3). Every great blessing begins with a great sacrifice, a great severance, a great dispossessing.

3. The open heart will be filled. "Open wide your mouth and I will fill it" (Psalm 81:10b). We know what it is for the flower-cup to close its petals and also to open to the sunlight, the dew and the refreshing shower. The heart has its susceptibilities and receptive sensibilities, but often it is so tightened up with unbelief, doubt, fear and selfconsciousness that it cannot take in the love which God is waiting to pour out. Like the

mother who found her long-lost child after years of separation, the child could not recognize the mother, and as she tried to awaken its response and to pour out the full tides of her bursting heart and found no recognition, but only the dull stare of strangeness and suspicion, her heart broke in grief and agony. So the heart of God has more to give us than we can receive.

4. Again, we are called by waiting upon the Lord in prayer, and especially in continued and believing prayer. It was after they had waited upon the Lord that they were all filled with the Holy Ghost. Prayer is not only an asking but also a receiving. Many of us do not wait long enough before the Lord to get filled. You can take your breakfast in half an hour, but you cannot be filled with the Holy Spirit as quickly.

5. Service for God and for others is perhaps the most effectual condition of receiving continually the fullness of the Spirit. As we pour out the blessing God will pour it in. And our blessing should always be twice blessed.

> Letting go is twice possessing.
> Would you double every blessing,
> Pass it on.

Above all the best way to be filled with the Spirit is to be true to the great trust for which He was given—the evangelization of the world. "But you will receive power when the Holy Spirit comes on you; and you will be my witnesses . . .

to the ends of the earth" (Acts 1:8). Perhaps this is the secret of our poverty—that we have tried to hoard our blessing, and let the world perish through our selfishness. "Freely you have received, freely give" (Matthew 10:8b).

> My soul, let down the empty vessels
> Of all thy need and sin and sorrow
> Into the Well of God's Great Fullness.
> And of His boundless blessing borrow.
>
> And most of all, He loves to help us
> To bless and help our needy brother;
> He answers first the prayers we offer
> Not for ourselves, but one another.
>
> And oh, with such a Friend behind us
> Let us not fear to scatter 'round us
> His grace to all the lost and suffering,
> And share with them the love that found us!

Thirty-first Day

SINNING AGAINST THE HOLY GHOST

And do not grieve the Holy Spirit of God.
(Ephesians 4:30)

Perhaps it is because the Holy Spirit is the gentlest of beings that the Lord Jesus has pronounced such awful penalties against those who sin against the Holy Ghost.

Everything that grieves the Holy Spirit is not necessarily to be construed as that one dreadful thing which the Scriptures call the sin against the Holy Spirit, which "will not be forgiven." But when we once begin to descend the awful incline of evil we never know where we are going to end. Therefore let us guard against the very beginnings of all that might lead to that dreadful attitude which the apostle describes when He says

130

"[They have] insulted the Spirit of grace"
(Hebrews 10:29b).

We may quench the Spirit. This perhaps has
reference rather to His public work in the
Church of God and the hearts of others than to
His particular dealings with our own soul. We
may discourage the work of the Spirit and the
liberty of worship and testimony by our harshness
and criticism. We may ourselves through timidity
or disobedience fail to obey His impulses in our
own hearts to testify for Him or to speak to
others about their souls. The minister of Christ
may quench the Spirit by worldly and sensational
themes, and by discouraging the Spirit of prayer,
separation and revival in the church. The Spirit is
quenched by worldliness, fashion and sinful
pleasure. The Spirit is quenched by error,
fanaticism and ecclesiastical pride. The cultiva-
tion of secular music and ambitious oratory, instead   of   humble   heart   searching   and
soul-winning—these things quench the Holy
Ghost. Nothing more quenches His reviving
power than strife, controversy, evil speaking and
division among the people of God.

Frivolous conversation in connection with the
house of God and sacred things often drives away
the convicting influence of the Holy Ghost from
others' hearts. A wife was laughing on her way
from church to her husband about some of the
peculiarities of the preacher. Suddenly she felt his
arm trembling and as she looked into his face the
tears were falling and he said, "pray for me. I have

seen myself tonight as I never have before." We may quench the Spirit in our church, we may quench the Spirit in our children and have the blood of souls in our hands forever.

Again the Scriptures speak of "grieving" the Holy Spirit. How gently this figure represents Him, not angry but pained. We may grieve Him by our doubts and fears. We may grieve Him by holding back some reserve in our consecration. We may grieve Him by disobedience and willfulness. We may grieve Him by coming short of the fullness of His blessing. We may grieve Him by a divided heart and the idolatry of earthly pleasures and affections. We may grieve Him by the neglect of His word. We may grieve Him by our lack of love to Jesus whom He always seeks supremely to honor and for whose rights He is jealous. We may grieve Him when we cherish bitterness toward our brethren and it is of this especially that the apostle says "Get rid of all bitterness, rage and anger, brawling and slander, along with every form of malice" (Ephesians 4:31). "And do not grieve the Holy Spirit of God, with whom you were sealed for the day of redemption" (4:30). And we may grieve Him by our spiritual selfishness, by praying only for our own needs and by letting the world perish in its ignorance and sin while we hear the gospel and neglect the cry of our brother.

But there is something worse than this. To some persons God had to say in days of old "You always resist the Holy Spirit!" The sinner resists

Him when he tries to shake off religious impressions and escape conviction of sin or procrastinate decision for Christ. He may do it very politely and intend at some "convenient season" to take up the matter again, but all the same the Holy Spirit recognizes it as rejection, refusal and insult. Therefore we read "So, as the Holy Spirit says: 'Today, if you hear His voice, do not harden your hearts' " (Hebrews 3:7–8a).

It is possible to do this by an imperceptible process as when a piece of iron is heated and cooled again and again until it corrodes and falls to pieces. The temper has been burned out of it, and there is nothing left but the dross. God says of some souls, "They are called rejected silver, because the Lord has rejected them" (Jeremiah 6:30). We never can tell when for the last time we are saying *No* to God and He is giving us the final invitation. Just because the Spirit is so gentle, patient, long-suffering and forgetful of His own honor and glory, therefore God has said "How much more severely do you think a man deserves to be punished who has trampled the Son of God under foot, who has treated as an unholy thing the blood of the covenant that sanctified him, and who has insulted the Spirit of grace" (Hebrews 10:29)?

Payson of Portland once said to a young friend who had come to speak to him about a slight religious impression that he had begun to feel "A little cord has dropped from heaven and for a moment touched your shoulder. It is so fine that you can scarcely feel it. Dear friend, grasp it quickly, for it is fastened to the throne of God and is perhaps for you the last strand of saving grace."

Books by Dr. A.B. Simpson:
The Best of A.B. Simpson
Christ in the Tabernacle
The Christ Life
The Self-Life and the Christ-Life
The Cross of Christ
Danger Lines in the Deeper Life
Days of Heaven on Earth
The Fourfold Gospel
The Gentle Love of the Holy Spirit
The Gospel of Healing
The Holy Spirit Vol. 1
The Holy Spirit Vol. 2
A Larger Christian Life
The Life of Prayer
Missionary Messages
The Names of Jesus
Wholly Sanctified